LIFE *on the*
FAMILY FARM

LIFE *on the* FAMILY FARM

Under an Open Heaven

Tom Heck

LIFE SENTENCE
Publishing, LLC

Scripture quotations from The Authorized (King James) Version. Rights in the Authorized Version in the United Kingdom are vested in the Crown. Reproduced by permission of the Crown's patentee, Cambridge University Press

Cover Design: Amber Burger

Editor: Sheila Wilkinson

www.lifesentencepublishing.com

Like us on Facebook

Visit Tom's website: www.tomheckfarm.com

Life on the Family Farm – Tom Heck

Printed in the United States of America

First edition published 2014

LIFE SENTENCE Publishing books are available at discounted prices for ministries and other outreach.

Find out more by contacting us at info@lifesentencepublishing.com

LIFE SENTENCE Publishing and its logo are trademarks of

LIFE SENTENCE Publishing, LLC
P.O. Box 652
Abbotsford, WI 54405

Paperback ISBN: 978-1-62245-159-3

Ebook ISBN: 978-1-62245-160-9

10 9 8 7 6 5 4 3 2 1

This book is available from www.amazon.com, Barnes & Noble, and your local Christian bookstore.

Share this book on Facebook:

Contents

Since my children were very young, I would tell them stories to bless, encourage and build character in them. They greatly loved my stories and always wanted to hear more of them.

A few years ago, I took it a step further and started writing for newspapers across America. I love sharing my life adventures with my readers. From the hundreds of responses I've received from so many people, it's obvious they enjoy my true stories just as much as my children did and still do!

This book is the accumulation of my stories written over a four year time period, between 2010 and 2014, appearing in the same order they were written.

I hope you enjoy and are blessed by these stories as much as my past readers have been.

ONE

Dinosaur Eggs

Spring has fully come to our farm here in northwestern Wisconsin after another long winter. Here in the north country, we always look forward to spring with all of its wonders, challenges and extra work. It's really nice to have all the deep snow gone and not to have that very cold Canadian air blowing in here.

It's nice to turn the young stock out on lush green pastures and see them run and kick up their heels and graze contentedly. Before we do that though, we go around and check and fix all the fences so we don't have any "great escapes." We've had a couple of them in the past and the cattle think they're great fun. They run and kick up their heels exploring their new territory, greatly enjoying their new freedom. When they're in this mindset, they can be awfully hard to round up and get back into their proper places. So we try to have all the fences up to par before we turn the cattle out to pasture to avoid any "great escapes," as we like to call them.

Another part of spring on the farm is working the land and planting the crops. With this comes the exciting part: finding dinosaur eggs. Sometimes ones that weigh well over a hundred pounds! Yes, you read that right. Occasionally we will find an exceptionally large one that we have to get the skid loader for.

The skid loader is great for digging them out and carrying them off the field. Well, if you haven't figured it out by now, I'm talking about rock-picking.

I know many farmers do a lot of grumbling and complaining about rocks and picking them – or worse yet, leaving them in their fields and then busting up their machinery on them. But we look at it differently.

We bought our farm in March of 1991 and every spring since then we have picked rocks. We do it the old fashioned way – by hand. We choose to enjoy it. Yes, it is hard, dirty work; but when you see the field picked clean, there is a real satisfaction in a hard job well done.

My wife and I were so extremely blessed years ago to get our own farm that we have always been so thankful to our Lord for it. We count it a privilege that we can have our own farm to farm and pick rocks on. We don't complain about it, we are thankful to be so blessed.

Now rock-picking is hard work, but we choose to make it fun. We wanted to keep a good attitude ourselves and set a good example for our young children. It's continued all these years. And even after many years, we all have fun with it.

Where did the dinosaur egg idea come from, you ask? Well, shortly after we bought this farm, we had the TV on one morning while we ate breakfast. The show had a world-renowned scientist on who had excavated many dinosaurs and had even found some fossilized dinosaur eggs in China. By using ultrasound, he found that one of the eggs had two embryos in it. They were hard rocks that weighed, I would guess, about ten pounds each. So after seeing this, when we found large egg-shaped rocks, we would call them "dinosaur eggs!" If we found a few large ones together we would call it a dinosaur nest. Then while we were picking it up, we would say, "You'd better watch your back side in case the mother dinosaur comes and finds you destroying her nest!" If the eggs were really large, "You had better be real careful, because just think how large that dinosaur must be." It would always draw some laughs and fun comments. And it would always make the work go better.

Another fun part of rock-picking was when we would pick the fields next to the woods. Our woods have loads of beautiful wild spring flowers in them that the kids would enjoy picking for their mom.

So no matter what the work is on the farm, or wherever you work, you can choose whether you want to enjoy it like we do, or you can grumble and complain about it. I know from personal experience and from seeing other people in both positions, it is far better to enjoy your work than to do the other. I know it is much more pleasing in the Lord's eyes also. So yes, enjoy your farming, the cattle on the fresh green pastures, hopefully staying in the fences, and even your rock-picking – and especially your family.

Two

Gone Fishing

W e pick rocks here on our farm the old-fashioned way. As a reward, I bless my family for all the hard work they put in rock-picking by buying them all fishing licenses. Then several times throughout the summer, I take them fishing.

A number of years ago, I bought a small, used, four-person boat. I did not have a lot of money to spend on one, so I bought a cheap one that has no motor on it. We get great exercise rowing it around the lake. It also came without a trailer, so we load it on our old farm pickup to haul it around. As I said, we bought a cheap one that we could afford. But we've gotten loads of pleasure out of it over the years. We take it to some small, backwoods lakes in the area.

Now I will be the first one to tell you that I know very little about fishing, but I do know how to put an angleworm on a fish hook. We usually catch some nice bluegills, a few crappies and a few bass. We sure have a lot of fun doing it. It is very nice and relaxing to take a few hours off between morning and evening milkings and just get off the farm and out to a beautiful, quiet lake with woods all around it, with our fishing poles. And then when your bobber goes way under and you have a tight line, it's pure excitement and wonderful.

I asked my daughter Catherine the other day, what lake she wanted to go to first this year. She replied, "To the lake where our two big ones got away last year!" Catherine hooked a really large fish last year. It took her line way deep, and then it went slack. She reeled it in to find her fish hook had busted in two. What a disappointment. But it was sure fun while it lasted!

I also had the largest fish that I ever hooked in my life at that same lake last year. It was a beautiful, large bass. I got so excited that I pulled too hard on my line and busted the line. I should have played him more easily. I guess after having picked all those rocks and building up my muscles, I figured I could just yank him in like a rock, but it didn't work that way! So it looks like we will be going back to that lake, trying to catch our two big ones that got away last year.

After a day of fishing, we look forward to a meal of fried fish when we're through with the evening milking. It is impossible to buy fish in a store that tastes as good as those do.

There are also other advantages to fishing. We take some of the bluegills and put them in our big cow water tank. They make excellent tank cleaners! Also, the cows find them very interesting to look at. Once when a milk inspector was here and noticed the fish in my cow water tank, I thought I was going to be in big trouble. I told him that they help to keep the tank clean, and that the kids really liked them in there. He replied, "It's an excellent idea, but you need more of them in there!" Boy, was I surprised and relieved by his comment. So after that, we got more fish in there, and the tank did get a lot cleaner.

The kids also really like to treat their favorite cats to a few small fish.

Some people are so busy working they don't have time to take their families fishing or to other fun things. It's farm, work, money or self, for many. It results in disappointing marriages and family life. I'm glad I've learned how to take a few hours off now and then with my family, to bless them and enjoy them. In the end, I am greatly blessed, even if it means I walk by a large rattlesnake sunning itself on the rocks by the lake shore, or the biggest thing I've ever caught is a large snapping turtle!

THREE

Independence Day

As I was out cutting hay recently, I was looking at the lush hayfields, the nice straight-rowed cornfields and the beautiful woods in the distance. I was in awe at how beautiful God, the Creator, made this all. The Bible tells us that the creation declares God's glory. The longer I live, the more amazed I am at the handiwork of God. Only a truly loving God would have created such a beautiful world for mankind.

It was about that time that a large wild turkey flew out of the hay close to my hay cutter. When one of those big birds explode out of the tall hay next to the rear tire on my tractor, just in front of my discbine, it almost makes me jump out of the tractor seat! They are one huge bird. At times, cutting hay can be very exciting!

We usually are busy putting up second crop hay around July 4th, Independence Day. We always take time to look towards town on that evening though, to watch the fireworks going off over the city and the ones our neighbors put up also. It is a time to thank God and celebrate the birthday of America and thank Him for all the liberties and freedoms we have been blessed with.

It was on March 23, 1775, that Patrick Henry gave his famous speech in the Virginia House of Burgesses in which he said, "Is life so dear, or peace so sweet, as to be purchased at the price of chains and slavery? Forbid it, Almighty God! I know not what course others may take, but as for me, give me liberty or give me death!"

Many of the Founding Fathers of our country knew it would cost them their fortunes as well as their own lives. Many of them had their blood shed so that America would be a free nation. Why? So that they could worship and serve God in freedom as they felt He was leading them to do. They did not shed their blood so they could be rich or famous, or so they could live in all kinds of sinful pleasures. They knew if they honored God, He would honor them. The price they paid was very high. We today are privileged to enjoy the tremendous freedoms they purchased.

Down through the history of this country, many men and women have stood and fought to maintain the great freedoms and ideals that America has stood for. Even today, we have many in the Army, Marines, Air Force, Coast Guard and National Guard serving on the front lines to keep our country free and to protect us. We owe all of these defenders of freedom a great debt of gratitude for all they are doing for us back here on the home front. So I say to any service person reading this, "Thank you very much for all you go through for us back here." Also, we say "Thank you very much" to the many who have come back that are in Veterans' hospitals and who live among us, some with serious disabilities they have suffered. We think of you often and remember you in our prayers.

We each need to be thankful to God and to them for the country we have today. We each need to worship and serve God as He leads us to. Not to get rich or famous, but to willingly do what He has called us to do. We have great liberties and freedoms today to use wisely – not for all kinds of sinful pleasures.

So as we work on the farm here and watch the fireworks, we will remember the great sacrifices our Founding Fathers paid and how the Lord honored and blessed them so that we could have a free country in which to serve Him.

FOUR

Rattlesnakes – Part 1

My grandfather was Paul K. Heck of Mondovi, Wisconsin. My mind always goes back to him around this time of year. He was born on July 14, 1898, west of Mondovi in Canton township. He lived to be about ninety-five years old. For many years he dairy-farmed northwest of Mondovi in what is known as German Valley. The early settlers in that valley were all of German ancestry; that's how the valley got its name. My grandfather farmed there many years before moving into Mondovi to live. Oftentimes in my single adult years, after milking my parents' dairy cows in the evening, I would go to my grandparents' home and visit with them. They had excellent memories and such a wealth of information from years gone by. The following account is one that my grandfather told me one evening that I'll probably remember the rest of my life. I'll do my best to retell it here now.

My grandfather had a friend many years ago who hunted rattlesnakes! He hunted many of them in the area along Highways 37 and 35 between Mondovi and Alma, especially down through the Alma area. The Buffalo River runs along Highway 37 and flows into the mighty Mississippi River just north of Alma. There are many large hills and magnificent bluffs along these rivers, particularly in the Alma area. Some of the bluffs I have been told are over five hundred feet tall. Some of them go right straight up with the lower parts of them covered with trees and the upper parts having huge rock faces with some grass growing on them. These beautiful bluffs with the great Mississippi River flowing beyond them are a real sight to behold. I think of the Bible verse that says, "The creation declares the glory of God." Only God could create such a masterpiece.

These many thousands of acres of river bottomland surrounded by thousands of acres of impressive bluffs were and are premium rattlesnake country – some of the best in the world. In the early to mid-1900s there was a very large population of these snakes in that area. They were a dangerous problem to all the people living there. Sometimes farmers would go to their warm barns early on cold mornings only to find a rattlesnake curled up in there. That would get the farmer fully awake really fast. Hopefully he would find it before his cats or cattle did. If not, he would oftentimes end up with a dead animal. During hot weather the snakes would sometimes seek the shade under the steps or porch of the house. Imagine the wife going down the porch steps and having a rattlesnake start to rattle at her a few feet away! If a person got bit by one, he had to get to a doctor fast or cut himself and try to get most of the venom out or else it would mean death to him.

With such a dangerous snake problem on their hands, Buffalo County put a sizable bounty on rattlesnakes. A number of men became excellent rattlesnake hunters and made good money doing it, especially during the Great Depression. Most of the time the hunters hunted on the high parts of the bluffs in and around all of the rocks. The snakes liked to sun themselves up there on the rocks, and they also had their dens in the rocks. Usually a man would hunt them all by himself. My grandfather's friend would oftentimes get a few snakes in a good day of hunting. He would kill the snakes and cut the rattles off the end of their tails, then take the rattles and turn them in to collect the bounty money.

There was another way to make money on them too. For a number of years, I was told, some of the restaurants in Alma would buy some of the larger snakes and serve them for dinner! I guess it was considered kind of a delicacy, and many people ate them. That is one I would definitely "pass" on though.

One sunny day after World War II, my grandfather's friend was hunting rattlers high on a bluff in the rocks and crevices. Now when he hunted snakes, he kept his eyes and ears really open, looking for them. The snakes could blend into the rocks, grass and brushy areas real easy, so a lot of times the snakes saw him before he saw them. When a snake saw him close by, it would start to rattle its tail. He would hear it and step in close and kill it. He carried a strong stick that was four to five feet long. He'd swing it, hit the snake in the head, and kill it. On this particular day he was in a rocky area that was pretty level. All of a sudden he heard a snake rattle on one side of him. Then he heard another one rattle on the other side of him, and then another one, and yet another one! He was surrounded by four very upset rattlesnakes, one on each side of him. As Grandpa told the story, I started to wonder who was really being hunted here.

The man realized he was in an extremely dangerous situation. If he got bit by two or three of these snakes, being way up on the bluff all alone, far from help, he was as good as a dead man. He was a very experienced hunter though and realized he had to stay calm. He quickly eyed up the situation and came up with a plan. He decided to call up the US Marines. He figured if they could take care of the Japanese soldiers at Okinawa, they could take care of a bunch of rattlesnakes. No, I'm just kidding, but he probably wished that he could have done it. I know I would have!

Rattlesnakes – Part 2

This fellow was rattlesnake hunting on the bluffs along the Mississippi River near Alma, Wisconsin. He was high on a bluff when all of a sudden he heard the rattle of a snake near him, then realized he was surrounded by four very upset rattlesnakes, one on each side of him.

He sized up the situation and quickly came up with a plan. He decided to turn in a circle on one foot as fast as he could, swinging his stick, trying to get all four snakes in one swinging action in a matter of one or two seconds. He knew the odds were against him, but he didn't see any other choice. He swung – and all I can say is that the Lord was with him. He killed all four snakes. He cut the rattles off all four and headed for home, calling it a day. I think his getting all four snakes in one swing was a far greater accomplishment than any golfer that ever shot a hole in one! He did say, however, that over his many years of hunting rattlesnakes, he did get bit twice; but he got medical attention and lived to tell about it.

Over the years though, because of the heavy hunter pressure on them, the snake population greatly declined. The bounty system had worked, and most people were very thankful with the results. The hunters who made most of their money off the snakes saw their livelihood dwindling greatly. Some came up with a very evil solution. They would find a rattlesnake and pin it to the earth. Then they would cut its rattles off and let it go. In time it would grow back new rattles on its tail and reproduce more snakes. A rattlesnake without its rattles is an extremely dangerous snake. People would walk right up to them and get no warning from the snake and be bitten by them. It is real sad to think that some snake hunters would do this for the love of money, thus stealing from the taxpayers and endangering the lives of other people. The Bible is most certainly correct when it says, "The love of money is the root of all evil." We all need to guard our hearts from the love of money and make sure we live honest before the Lord and all men.

The Bible also refers to the devil as the serpent or snake. And, just like a rattlesnake without a rattle, the devil is a deceiver, but Jesus crushed that snake's head at Calvary so that we could have victory over him. More than that, we can have a personal relationship with God and make heaven our home some day when we die. One day I read a book about an all-loving God who sent His Son Jesus to Calvary to die and pay the price for my sins, so I could be forgiven and redeemed unto Him. I got down on my knees that day in my bedroom and asked Him to forgive me and to be Lord of my life. I committed to follow Him and live for Him all the rest of my life. If you have never done this, I cannot urge you strongly enough to do it today. You will never regret it. I haven't. I only wish I would have done it sooner.

Bringing the Cows Home

In the summer time on our farm, we normally put the cows out to pasture after the evening milking. They really like going out at night when it's cooler. In the hot, sunny daytime they would rather stay in the barn in the shade where we have the fans running. They have all the feed and cold, fresh water right in front of them, so they can eat and drink to their hearts' content.

We have tried putting them out both day and night, but they don't like that. When we have done it, they will stand just outside of the barn looking at us and mooing. They won't go out to the pasture. So we end up opening up the barn, and they come rushing back in. Cows have a mind of their own, and they know what they want – and they let you know it too.

We have a feeder wagon just outside of the barn that we put feed on for them. We also have a large water tank out there full of fresh, cold water. We normally have some blue gills and crappies in it to help keep the tank clean. The cows, along with us, find the fish very entertaining. Oftentimes the cows will stand there and watch them swimming back and forth. Sometimes a fish will be half sleeping or day dreaming on top of the water. The cows can't resist one of them. Curiosity always wins out. A cow will stick her big nose up to the fish to smell it and check it out. When that happens, the fish will wake up, make a splash, and dive for the deep. All the cows around the water tank will jump back in surprise. This hasn't happened just a couple times, but hundreds of times over the years. Every time we see it happen, we just bust out laughing. It's amazing the effect a little two-ounce fish can have on 1,400-pound cows!

Once the cows are done with eating at the feeder wagon and playing with the fish, they head out to pasture. The younger ones oftentimes run out kicking up their heels and racing each other to the far end of the pasture. There's just something about getting there first to check it out. The older cows simply walk out, taking their good old time and enjoying it. This is their "fun time" of once again checking out the pasture and interacting with one another. Then they will graze to their hearts' content and lie down in the tall green grass to rest overnight. They really like the fresh air, exercise and the lush green grass. Fresh air and exercise is excellent for people, too. Get out and enjoy the beautiful world that God has put around you, like the cows do. It will be good for you as well.

Then morning comes. Somebody gets to go out to the pasture and bring the cows in for the morning milking. This is the job my wife Joanne greatly enjoys. She insists on doing it most of the time. Everything is so quiet and peaceful early in the morning, as the sun is coming up in the east. This is one of her favorite times to seek God and pray. Proverbs 8:17 says, "Those that seek me early shall find me."

As you go out in our cow pasture, there's a large steep hill that's flat on top at the south end of the pasture. As you head north, there's a large valley, followed by a smaller hill to the north of that. From the top of the large southern hill, you have a bird's eye view of the whole pasture.

Now, each cow has her own name, and she knows it. Normally Joanne climbs the large southern hill when she goes to bring the cows in. The cows will be lying contentedly spread out over the entire pasture. She will start calling each one by name: Molly, Bessie, Honey, Lucy, Cutie and so forth. When they hear their names called, they stand up. They will stretch, and then they start walking to the barn. There are some cows though who won't get up until their name is called. This is how we bring our cows up for milking. It's something how intelligent God made the cows, that each one knows her name. What's more amazing yet is how God made every person on this earth, and He knows each one by name. Only a truly loving, caring God would do something like that.

Streaked Gophers

As a farmer, I really appreciate nice smooth fields. But there are a couple of things that will destroy a really nice hayfield and sometimes good machinery too. They are called streaked gophers and pocket gophers. Streaked gophers, or as some people call them, thirteen-striped ground squirrels, are very intelligent animals, and they have many enemies.

A streaked gopher will dig anywhere from one to ten different holes or tunnels in the earth to live in. When they dig a tunnel, they end up making a mound of dirt just outside of it. Then you know what happens next? Foxes, coyotes, or worse yet, earth movers come along looking for a nice juicy meal. What's an earth mover, you ask? A badger. A badger will dig huge holes, putting out wheelbarrows full of dirt. No other animal can dig like a badger.

All these diggers can smell the gopher down in its tunnel, so they start digging after it. The gopher hears them and fears their coming, so the gopher starts digging away from it, pushing the dirt behind itself in its tunnel. When this happens, the fox, coyote or badger knows it's close to the gopher. Sometimes just inches away, so that they dig even harder, trying to get that nice tasty meal. Normally though, the gopher can stay a few inches ahead of them, so eventually they quit pursuing it and decide to come back another night and try again. That does wonders for the hayfield!

The results are that the farmer ends up getting a real bumpy ride on his tractor when he is out working in his hayfield. It doesn't do his machinery any good either. When his hay cutter cuts through these dirt mounds, it's awful hard on its sickle or knives. It will dull them real fast and sometimes break them. When the farmer harvests his hay a day or two later, all those mounds and holes are hard on the equipment as well. I have seen some equipment actually totaled out from them.

So, farmers really like to get rid of these gophers, but it takes a fair bit of time and work to do it. Therefore a lot of farmers just put up with them and hope for the best. There's a great solution for this gopher problem though – kids. I remember back about forty years ago when I was a young kid on my parents' dairy farm. I was out in my dad's cornfield a few days after he planted it. To my surprise I saw a streaked gopher had gone down several rows of corn for thirty to fifty feet digging out every kernel of corn and eating it. The Creator made these cute little animals very smart.

Well, I went home and told my dad what that gopher had done. He wasn't too happy about it. He knew that gopher would continue to dig up more of his corn and eat it. In the fall that cornfield would have a spot in it, with no corn to harvest.

My dad had a brilliant idea. He told me that I should take a trap out there and catch it. If I caught it, he would give me a nickel. Now I hadn't trapped gophers before; but that sounded like fun, and I could earn a whole nickel. Within hours, I had the gopher and the nickel. My dad was amazed at how well and fast his idea worked. So then he had another great idea. He offered me a nickel for every streaked gopher I caught off his farm that summer. No streaked gopher was safe!

All summer long I kept my eyes open for gopher holes in

the cornfields, hayfields and pastures. Whenever I found one, it didn't take me long to get a trap there. By the end of the summer, I had gotten sixty-some streaked gophers. That was over three dollars. I was making money! But I was making a lot more. I was learning to be responsible and to be self-motivated. Was it work? Not really. I greatly enjoyed it. It was also challenging. I wouldn't always catch the gopher on the first try, or even the second try. Some were really sneaky and wise, so it taught me diligence to keep after them until I would catch them. There were also other rewards. I greatly enjoyed roaming the fields and pastures, the hills and marshes, taking in all of God's creation. I also had the fun of treating my favorite barn cats. They loved gophers.

The Bible tells us that parents are to teach and train their children in the way that they are to go. A big part of that is giving them work and teaching them responsibility. Parents need to set a good example before their children and then hold them responsible. Sometimes putting a little reward out for a job well done doesn't hurt either.

I am sure my dad thought he got the best end of the deal – getting rid of sixty-some streaked gophers for just over three dollars. But I know differently. I got the best end of the deal. Parents, don't short-change your kids. Give them work and responsibility. Some day they will thank you for it.

EIGHT

The Aerial Show

One of the jobs that I really enjoy doing on the farm here in the summer time is cutting hay. It is wonderful to get out in God's beautiful creation. There's always an exciting, beautiful aerial show to watch. It amazes me how our Creator made so many unique and beautiful birds. There are many different birds that are attracted to my hayfields.

The ones that are out there in large numbers are the red-winged blackbirds. Their bright red wing patches on the rest of their black bodies really make them stand out. I have an old fence post by a certain field road that red-winged blackbirds love to sit on and sing out their beautiful songs. So over time, I ended up calling this particular field road "Blackbird Road."

I also have another really sharp beautiful small bird out there called the bobolink. When I was a young kid, I called them skunk birds. They are mostly black with white patches or stripes of white on their wings and backs, kind of like a skunk. But they certainly don't smell like a skunk! They also sing out a very beautiful song. They migrate all the way down to central South America late in the summer to overwinter down there. Then in the spring, they come all the way back up here. It amazes me the wisdom and intelligence God gave these little birds. It is true that God cares for everything.

These two particular species of birds live in my hayfields. They eat lots of bugs and insects, along with an occasional earthworm.

Then I have the larger birds living in my woods that come to visit when I am out there cutting hay. Why do they come and visit then, you ask? Because they like me so much that they just have to come and say, "Hello." No, I am just teasing; but they most certainly do come. When I am out in the hayfield cutting hay with my discbine, usually a few field mice, and once in a while a streaked gopher, will get killed by it. In come the birds of prey for a free meal like the US Air Force on a bombing mission, sometimes landing within feet of my discbine.

The crows will come in first, looking for dead mice, bugs and insects. When they find a mouse, they will usually carry it off to their nest high up in some tree in the woods to feed to their young ones. The blackbirds will seek to attack the crows in the air, peck at them, and sometimes hurt them. They do this to try and keep them out of their territory. The blackbirds protect their young ones and their food supply this way. The blackbirds can out maneuver the crows because they are smaller. Oftentimes four or five blackbirds will attack a single crow in the air, trying to drive it out of their hayfield.

Next we get even bigger birds coming, looking for free meals. They are the hawks. Now when the crows see them coming, they try to ambush them in the air and drive them away. The crows, like the blackbirds, don't want to share the goodies with anybody else. On occasion, I have seen blackbirds attacking crows which are attacking hawks all at the same time. It can be an incredible aerial show.

Once in a while, I see a great, majestic bald eagle in my hayfield. A couple times I have gotten within thirty or forty feet of one of them. They are one incredible bird!

My favorite bird to watch though, when I am cutting hay, is

the peregrine falcon. These birds will go into a headfirst dive and get up to 180 miles per hour. Just a few feet before hitting the ground, they will spread out their wings to break their crash dive. They are excellent hunters, catching live mice, gophers, rats and snakes. The first time I saw one of these dive, it was heading to the earth so fast I thought there was no way it could pull out of its incredible dive. I was sure there was going to be a dead bird. But at the last split second, it put its wings out and had a hard landing. It caught the mouse; and after a little recovery time, took back off.

I find it very interesting and enjoyable watching all these birds. It does not surprise me that the US Air Force has named some of its aircraft after certain birds. I stand in awe at how our Creator has made all these birds so unique and special. You don't have to be out cutting hay, like I do, to enjoy the birds. Just get outside and look around you. You may well be amazed at what you see. God made each species of birds unique, just like He has made each and every person unique. Who could make the small bobolink so pretty and give it the ability to travel many thousands of miles, or who could make the falcon such a skillful hunter that dives at such incredible speeds, or who could make all the other birds each so unique in their ways? Only a very wise, loving God – the same one who created you and me. He made you very unique and special because He loves you so. The Bible tells us that He loves you much more than the birds. Matthew 10:31 says, "Ye are of more value than many sparrows." He has a wonderful plan for your life. If you will seek Him, He will reveal it to you.

NINE

The Raiders

They sneak in at night under the cover of darkness to do their stealing. They work quietly and quickly, doing their work, which they greatly enjoy. They seek to do a very thorough job. It doesn't pay to call the police because, No. 1 they won't catch them, and No. 2 if they did catch them, they wouldn't arrest them. Who are these thieves and what are they stealing, you ask? They are varmints raiding people's sweet corn patches around the country.

One of the patches they seek to raid is the one we plant on our farm. Now I know why they like to raid it. Nothing beats fresh sweet corn. Fresh ears of sweet corn roasted with plenty of butter and a little salt on them are absolutely delicious. When it's in season, Joanne, Catherine and Joshua usually eat two big ears each for dinner every day, while I have three. It is just so good!

The raiders think so too. They will come from far and wide to feast. These animals were endowed by their Creator with excellent noses. They can smell the sweet corn a long ways off. Then it's just a matter of following their noses to the sweet corn patch. Once they're there, the party begins. I have often seen on the following morning over a hundred ears they have ripped off the stalks and eaten. How they can eat so much I don't know.

They have an incredible appetite for sweet corn. I have heard from neighbors of mine how these raiders have eaten every single ear of corn in their patches. They didn't leave them one single ear. Usually when they tell me this, they are very upset about it. They went to all the work of planting it, only to get it all stolen from them.

Who are these raiders, you ask? Well, the first ones are the raccoons. If a single coon finds a delicious patch of sweet corn on a particular night, you can be assured he will invite all his relatives for the following night. They believe in sharing the treasure they have found with all their friends. I have seen coons leaving the sweet corn patch with their big overloaded bellies about dragging on the ground. When it comes to sweet corn, a coon doesn't know what the word "moderation" means.

The next worse ones are the skunks. Skunks really like sweet corn also. With their sharp claws and teeth, they too will eat a lot of sweet corn. The next ones on the list, which surprise a lot of people, are red fox. They usually sneak in and out in the middle of the night undetected; but they also eat sweet corn. I guess it helps balance their diet. The last ones on the list are opossums. Now we don't have a lot of them around here, so they are not near the problem that the others are.

You ask me, how do I know all this? From experience. We really value our sweet corn patch. We eat a lot of sweet corn fresh, and we also freeze a lot to eat the rest of the year. Catherine, Joshua and I pick the ears and husk them, and Joanne takes care of it from there. But if there's going to be any sweet corn for us, we have to control the raiders. Fortunately we are good trappers. Catherine and Joshua help me trap them. Over the years, we have caught lots of raccoons and skunks out of our patch, along with several red fox and a few opossums.

Now my daughter Catherine has a stuffed raccoon that she received from my sister years ago. It is her favorite stuffed animal and has taken on a life of its own. She named him "Coonie." Coonie always tells me that his relatives aren't stealing my sweet corn. They are just helping themselves. I tell him they had better help themselves some other place, if they know what's good for them. He tells me he tells them that, but sometimes their bellies overrule their brains, and they end up in my sweet corn patch anyway.

We don't exactly enjoy getting rid of these animals, but we know if we don't control them, we will not get any sweet corn. There are other things in life that we need to do also that we don't enjoy, but it is necessary. Whether it's disciplining a child or paying taxes or cleaning a bathroom. The big thing is to keep our attitudes right. If we do, we will enjoy life a lot more and be much more blessed. I know we are. We sure like our hot, buttered, lightly-salted ears of sweet corn for dinner. They are delicious.

TEN

Keep on Trying

Things don't always work out as a person plans. For years the hay head on the chopper that I own has continually given me problems shearing off bolts. It has been very frustrating. Oftentimes I would be going along chopping, and for no reason whatsoever, the shear bolt would shear off. The hay head would quit picking up the hay. I would have to stop and take two shields off the head. I would have to get two wrenches and a new bolt and put the new bolt in the head. Then I would put the shields back on and be in business again.

I learned over the years to carry these two certain wrenches along with a new supply of bolts and nuts in my chopper's tool box. I learned the manufacturer only made a couple thousand heads with this particular drive set-up on them. Farmers had a lot of trouble with them, so they redesigned the drive and solved the problem. That was very good, but I have one of the old heads with the old problem!

Finally, after years of putting up with it, I decided I had enough. I checked with my local machinery dealer and found out to replace that whole drive assembly with the new style would cost quite a bit of money. So I decided I would re-engineer it myself at my farm shop. My kids, Catherine and Joshua, were eager to help me with the project. It ended up being a little harder than what I thought, but we got it. When we finished, we test ran it, and it did just fine. We were all smiling and happy. We had the problem fixed – or so we thought.

Haying season came. I have about one-and-a-half acres of hay around my farm buildings here that I always cut first. I was really thankful for this because it would give me a good chance to check out my hay head under actual field conditions. Well, it worked perfect. I thanked the Lord for it and cut a large amount of hay for the next day.

The next day came bright, sunny and beautiful – a real hay-making day. I started chopping. I went about a hundred yards, and then my hay head quit working. Was I surprised and disappointed! Here I had this large amount of hay down, and I barely get started, and my hay head quits working.

Well, I got off the tractor and went back and took the two shields off. Nothing had busted, but it wouldn't stay in "drive." I did a little work on it and started chopping again. This time I went about a hundred feet, and it quit working again.

I went back again, took the two shields off, and looked at it. It was the same situation as the time before. I headed home with it to the farm shop. Catherine, Joshua and my wife Joanne all quickly came to see if they could help me. They are all super helpers. We prayed to God for wisdom in how to fix this. I ended up tightening a spring up and wedging a bolt into the drive part of it. This temporary fix worked for getting the rest of that hay crop off. I knew that I definitely had to fix it better before the next hay crop. Since then, I have redesigned it again, and now it works perfectly.

In life, things don't always work out and go as planned. They didn't for me with my chopper head. But as we looked to the Lord, we were able to keep our spirits and our tongues right. What a blessing! By so doing, we didn't hurt one another and sin against our Lord. By keeping on trying, God did bless us. We got our hay crop off, and we have an excellent working hay head today. As we look to the Lord, He always sees us through.

Eleven

Beautiful Twins

Every so often we have a special event happen on our farm. We never quite know for sure when these special events will occur, but generally, we have a pretty good idea. The cows let us know. What are these special events, you ask? A cow giving birth to a new calf. I have seen this occur countless times in my life, but the miracle of new life coming into the world never ceases to amaze me, especially when it happens on my own farm.

When a cow starts to "calve" – that is, to give birth to a new calf – we always like to keep an eye on her. Once in a while she can have complications giving birth, so we like to be available to help her if she needs it. We always try to be there to welcome the new arrival into the world. We don't want a single baby calf to die.

There are some calvings that end up being very unique, that we never forget. Once we had one happen here when Patience calved. Patience was starting to bring a calf. The water bag had already burst, but she was having trouble. It so happened that earlier that day I had put on a brand new shirt. It was the very first time I wore it to the barn.

I went into her with my hand and arm and found a big surprise. Twins! The problem was that they were tangled up with each other, so it was impossible for her to bring them forth. Without help, Patience and her twins would surely die. We had caught her in this situation at just the right time though. I went to work at untangling the twins. Two heads along with eight legs and two bodies can be a lot to untangle. Obviously, when they are in the cow, you cannot see them; so you have to feel around inside of her and figure out which legs go with which body. Then you need to untangle them.

You need to remember things are extremely crowded inside a cow's womb and that she is in labor straining to bring forth her babies. It makes for a very challenging situation. I always find myself praying to the Lord for wisdom and guidance in these situations.

I went to work untangling the calves. Then it happened. Patience strained hard. There was a second water bag in her that burst with great force. I and my brand new shirt got drenched. I turned to my wife and kids, who were there assisting me, and said, "It looks like my new shirt just got baptized into farming." We all just busted out laughing.

Well, I continued to work on them, and I got them untangled. We brought forth a beautiful heifer and bull calf, sister and brother, into the world. We cleaned the mucous out of their mouths and noses and made sure they got breathing good. We were all thanking the Lord that it had turned out so well despite the complications. A little later on, we made sure that they got some of their mother's milk to drink. We named the heifer "Pretty" and the bull "Buster."

Patience, Pretty and Buster all did very well after that. We do our utmost to give our animals here the very best care possible, but once in a great while a cow or calf will die. We all feel sad and sorrowful when that happens.

How much sadder and tragic it is when a person dies, especially a baby. We know from the Bible that God puts more value on an unborn human baby than he does on all the material wealth of the world. I do all I can to save an unborn calf from dying, and rightly so. Yet an unborn calf doesn't compare in value to an unborn child. It makes me cry when I hear of a mother who has her baby killed through abortion. How tragic. There are many married, loving couples that would love to adopt a baby from a mother who feels she cannot take care of it. If you would give your child a chance to live, I am sure some day down the road he/she would be very thankful to you for it. I know my calves Pretty and Buster were sure happy to be alive.

TWELVE

The Red Rose

Years ago when I dated my wife, I realized she was a very special person. It didn't take long for me to fall in love with her. After we were married, my love for her continued to grow. True love always seeks to bless the other person. Love gives.

Over the years, I have tried to bless my wife with things I know she really likes. Something my wife really, really likes are roses. So over the years, I have planted a number of roses here on our farm for my wife. If Joanne didn't like roses, I wouldn't have planted a single one!

One of the roses I planted is a very special rose. It has large, deep red, velvety flowers on it. They are the most gorgeous roses I have ever seen. I ordered it through a special catalog, and it cost me a pretty penny. But it was for my sweetheart, so it was well worth it, I thought.

When the UPS truck delivered my rose, I quickly planted it. It had a small root with about an eight-inch cane sticking out of the ground. I was really anticipating this one growing so that I could pick the beautiful roses for my precious wife. Things don't always go as planned, though. Sometimes they go terribly wrong.

A few days after I planted it, I was out by Champ's doghouse. Now Champ is a big, brown St. Bernard/black lab/collie mix that weighs well over a hundred pounds. I noticed a stick lying there that he had chewed all up. He does a real good job chewing things up. For some strange reason, it looked familiar, but I just passed it off.

I went to work, and after a few hours, it hit me. That was the red rose I had so tenderly planted for my wife! I went immediately and picked it up. It was in terrible shape. It looked totally hopeless. I was half brokenhearted over it, but what could I do? The only thing I knew to do was to take it back out there and plant it again. So I planted a dead stick into the ground because I didn't know what else to do.

After a couple of weeks, I remembered that the catalog company had a guarantee on their plants to grow. My rose wasn't growing, so I called them up. They informed me, though, that their guarantee did not cover dog attacks. So I was left with one expensive, chewed-up rose.

Over the summer I walked by that rose many times, but I just didn't have the heart to pull it out of the ground and throw it away. Then a small miracle happened. Almost four months after the dog attack, I was walking by the rose one day, and I noticed close to the ground two green leaves starting to appear. I was very surprised, to say the least. I had given it up for dead long ago.

Well, it lived. Now, for years, it has grown the most beautiful roses for me to give to my sweetheart. The other day I was driving my tractor in the driveway, and I saw a perfect red rose blossom on it. So I had to pick it and give it to my sweetheart. Of course, she greatly appreciated it.

I am sure glad that I didn't throw that rose into the garbage or brush pile after Champ chewed it up. I must admit I didn't have much faith in it growing, but I'm sure glad I replanted it. Like that chewed-up red rose, a person's life may be chewed up by sin, or a lot of bad decisions, or abuse and may seem totally hopeless. I know mine did. I also know that when Jesus came into my heart, He made something beautiful out of my life. I know He can do the same for you.

THIRTEEN

Baling the Bees

Years ago dairy farmers baled lots of hay during the hot summer months to feed to their cattle over the long winter months. When I was a young man, I used to go and help my uncle George sometimes during the summer months. He baled lots of hay. There was something that happened one day when he was baling hay that I will never forget.

He was out baling hay on a large level field. He always used his Farmall 560 tractor on the baler. That tractor did not have a cab on, so it was real easy to get on and off fast. That proved extremely important on this particular day. He had a very heavy crop of hay, so he had his tractor in a real low gear. The baler was working at full capacity to handle the large roll of hay. Fortunately, the baler had a thrower on it, so it threw the bales into the large hay wagon hooked behind it.

Uncle George was in the middle of the field when the attack came. In the roll of hay was a large swarm of bees. As the loud, noisy tractor and baler got to the swarm of bees, they were enraged. The tractor was running at full throttle, and the baler was picking up the hay along with the bees.

The bees attacked the baler, the tractor and my uncle. As I said before, it was a large swarm of bees. My uncle got stung by one or two of them and jumped off the tractor and ran about fifty feet away. Then he watched the show.

The tractor and baler kept going across the field baling hay. Don't ask me how the baler stayed exactly on the roll of hay. Tractors back then didn't have computerized autosteer like some of the new ones do today. But the tractor stayed perfectly on course.

Some of the bees really went after the baler, trying to sting it, and ended up getting into the baling chamber. A few bales of hay ended up getting bees in them for the cows to eat the following winter. Other bees attacked the noisy tractor. They tried to land on the loud, hot muffler to sting it. That didn't work out very good for them either. So eventually the ones that were left and were able to, flew away.

Once they were gone, my uncle went back to his tractor and got on it and kept right on baling. A bunch of angry bees was not going to stop my uncle George from doing his work. He finished baling that field of hay that day.

Several months later in the middle of the winter, one day he opened up some hay bales for his cows to eat with dead bees in them. He smiled as he remembered back to the day when he watched a driverless tractor and baler going across his field with a swarm of bees attacking it.

Adversity will come to all of us in our work at times – sometimes from totally unexpected sources, but that is no reason to quit. Quitters finish last. So keep on doing your work, being faithful in the work God has given you to do. In the end, you will be glad that you were. George was and so were his cows.

Tom baling hay on his own farm.

FOURTEEN

The Young Pilots

It's that time of year again, when a lot of young ones are getting their pilot licenses, or as some people might say, "their wings." We have quite a number of them on our farm here this year doing just that. It is really fun and sometimes a little scary to watch them start to fly. Once in a while one of them will crash into something; or worse yet, get killed. We hate to see this happen, but it's a part of growing up for them.

What am I talking about, you ask? Our friendly, little barn swallows are learning to fly. Every year in early May, our barn swallows travel thousands of miles from South America to come back here to live. They build their nests out of mud, locating them on the ceiling joists in my barn and under the eaves of my barn's roof. They line their new nests with feathers, cow hair and that nice hair that my big brown dog Champ sheds. They really like his soft hair in their nests.

We greatly enjoy our barn swallows, especially those that nest in our barn just two or three feet above our heads. The mother swallows will usually lay five eggs and then set on them for two to three weeks until they hatch. Then it's a heavy work load for Mom and Dad. They fly around swooping and diving, catching all kinds of flies and insects to feed their young families. One of their favorite insects to eat are mosquitoes, for which I am very thankful. God made these birds, which are only five to seven inches long, to do very important work.

As the little birds grow, the nest gets more and more crowded for them. After a few weeks, the nest is bulging at the seams with almost fully-grown swallows. This is really a fun stage for them and us. They will all be peering down at us, watching us milk our cows and do our other barn chores. Of course, we keep looking up and enjoy our cute feathered friends.

Then the day comes when they are old enough to start to fly. Dad and Mom fly around the nest talking to them in their own unique language, encouraging them one by one to take the big step of faith out of their little secure nest and try out their new wings. One by one they will do this with Dad and Mom flying next to them. The parents fly alongside and instruct the new flyer in how to do it.

It's also a dangerous time for them because once in a while they will crash into something and end up on the barn floor or earth. Why is this so dangerous, you ask? Barn cats! Every once in a while a cat will catch one of these birds and have it for dinner. We will sometimes find a small pile of swallow feathers lying around afterwards that tells the story.

It's fun watching these birds learn to fly and gain their independence. They can fly and maneuver in the air better than any aircraft man has built. The Creator sure knew how to design these little flyers. When these little birds leave their nests, we say to each other that they are getting their "pilot licenses." The cats are always watching with great interest, too.

The other day I was feeding my cows in the barn when I walked by one of my window wells that had a young pilot helplessly fluttering against the window. If a cat found it like that, it would surely be a dead bird. I gently caught it in my hands and carried it out in front of my barn and let it go. The last I saw, it was flying over my clover hayfield. I was glad I could help the little fellow out. It made my day, and I'm sure it must have made his also.

God made the barn swallows very unique and special. The Bible tells us He cares for the birds. I was happy and blessed that I could care for the little one the other day. The Bible also tells us that He cares for you much more than the birds. If you will trust Him and turn your life over to Him, He will take good care of you, just like I did with the new little pilot the other day.

Young barn swallows about to go on their first flight.

FIFTEEN

Delicious Corn

I t's that time of year again. It's one of the favorite times of the year for cows on our farm here. They look forward to it almost like a child looks forward to their birthday and all the good presents they will receive. What are they looking forward to, you ask? Fresh corn harvest. It all starts with our sweet corn. We harvest the delicious ears for ourselves, then take a corn knife and cut the cornstalks off. Joshua and Catherine load our old wheelbarrow heaping full with them. Then it's off to the barn with it.

Now my cows have big, powerful noses on them. They can smell the sweet corn coming before they can even see it. They will start to moo gently and look to the south end of our barn where we bring our wheelbarrow. Then we carry large armfuls of it into the barn to distribute in front of them. Each cow in her stall eagerly awaits her three or four stalks of sweet corn – but it's so hard to wait for it!

Even though they have plenty of other feed in front of them, they strain and reach as far as they can to grab the stalks out of our arms before we can even give it to them. Or worse yet, they try to take it from their neighbor who just received hers. They will stick their big, powerful tongues out eight to ten inches and wrap them around a stalk like an octopus would one of its tentacles. In this situation, Bossy doesn't know what the word "patience" means.

Once all the cows have received their sweet cornstalks, the mooing stops, and it's pure delight. The cows are all in cow heaven, as they chew away on their sweet corn. Oftentimes we will see a cow start at the bottom of the stalk, holding it in her mouth, having it stick out five to six feet in front of her. She will start chewing away at it, working the stalk and all its leaves slowly into her mouth. Bossy will eat the whole stalk down this way. How she can hold the stalk, chew it and work the whole thing into her mouth this way, only using her mouth, amazes me. God made cows very unique, special creatures.

Their fresh-corn appetite doesn't stop here though. If I, or my neighbor, have a field of corn planted next to my cow pasture, the cows just have to help themselves. It's just irresistible. They will put their heads, along with their long necks, between two strands of wire and push as hard as they can to reach the outer row of corn. Once they reach it, out go their long, powerful tongues, wrapping them around the corn plants and either breaking the stalks off or pulling them out by the roots. Sometimes almost the whole row of corn along the pasture fence is missing by the time harvest rolls around. But if you look at my cows lying in the pasture, they look so innocent.

Then as the corn gets more mature, I start to chop it for the cows. They really like this because it's cut in small pieces so they can eat it a lot faster and easier. It is just so delicious to them. What do they do with all this good corn they eat, you ask? They turn it into delicious milk for us to drink and all kinds of tasty, nutritious dairy products, such as cheese, ice cream and butter.

There are a couple of very unique things about cows most people don't realize. One is that cows only have teeth on their bottom jaw. Their top jaw is real hard flesh, yet they can chew up grass, alfalfa and cornstalks with no problem. Another unique thing about a cow is that her stomach is made up of four different compartments. Each one plays a special part in digesting the feed a cow eats. God made cows unique and special in many ways. We try to take excellent care of our cows, and they bless us in return. God made each person unique and special too. He gave each one special talents and abilities for their own good and to use for His glory. He loves you far more than I do my cows. If you will follow Him, He will take better care of you than I do my cows. It's the best life possible. I know from experience.

Bossy eating her sweet corn stalk.

Sixteen

Ferocious Bears

We have some real good friends that greatly enjoy hunting on our land every year. They bless us in their friendship and in including us in their hunting. They hunt turkeys and deer out of our woods. Usually after a day of hunting, they will stop at our buildings here to tell us how their hunting went and show us what they got.

We are always extremely interested in their hunting adventures on our land. Once in a while when they have bagged a really nice one they just can't wait to get up here to the buildings to tell us about it. They will call us on their cell phones right from the woods. Isn't modern technology great?

Speaking of modern technology, they bring along their trail cameras and put them up. I didn't know what those things were until they introduced me to them and showed me how they work. It's a battery-powered camera with a motion sensor built into it, that they strap to a tree. When it senses motion, it takes a picture that it digitally records on a memory stick. It will record hundreds of pictures on a single stick.

Well, we were fascinated by these cameras and all the pictures that they recorded. So our hunter friends went and bought us one and gave it to us as a gift, which we really appreciated.

What is neat is that we can hook up our camera to our TV

and watch all the pictures on there in living color. Now, we don't watch much TV here because most of the stuff on it is so bad, but we sure enjoy watching our own "wildlife movies," as we like to call them.

A while back I put our camera out in our woods. I found a site I thought would be an excellent place to catch a lot of wildlife activity at. Was I ever right! I got hundreds of squirrels and raccoon pictures. I also got pictures of a number of different birds – some that I had never seen before in my life. What was more exciting though were the deer pictures that we got – a number of does with their fawns beside them.

Then what was most surprising were the black bears on it. Our camera is set to take one picture every minute when it senses motion. I put the camera in a grove of large oak trees figuring the wildlife would come to eat the acorns. Now for a while we had one big black bear coming to eat. But then a second large black bear found the spot also. These two bears didn't want to share the acorns with each other. They did not have any brotherly love. So, for at least fifteen minutes they scrapped it out with each other. The camera recorded the fight.

They were up and down, rolling around, making a mess of themselves and the area. I was glad I had the camera present and that I was a long ways away. Sometimes it's best to stay out of others' fights! The deer, raccoon and squirrels were a whole lot nicer. Sometimes we would have pictures of four or five of them sharing the acorns, eating to their hearts' content.

How good it is when people respect each other and walk in brotherly love also. When people act like the two bears, they usually make a mess of their own lives, as well as the lives of others. We would all do well to heed the Bible when it says to walk in love as Christ has loved us and given himself for us. I know from experience to walk in love is truly the best life possible.

Two black bears scrap it out in Tom Heck's woods.
The big bear on the left ended up winning the fight.

The Fireball Miracle

S ometimes the totally unexpected happens, and sometimes the totally unexpected is very bad. Such is what happened here a little bit ago. We had a great, productive day going here on the farm. It was the last day of baling hay for the year. With the abundant rain the Lord had given us this year, we were blessed with the largest hay crop ever on our farm. Our barn's haymow was already packed out full, and we were having to store this hay in part of the bedding mow. What a blessing to have so much good hay in storage to feed to our cattle in the coming winter months.

I went out early in the day and raked the hay up into large rolls of hay, and then went back to bale it. I'd bale a large load and bring it into the barn, where Joshua would unload it and then help Catherine mow it away. Since the hay was running heavy that day, we had more than I had expected, and we ended up getting late with our evening chores.

Joanne started our evening barn chores without us. As the kids and I were finishing up the very last of the hay that day, Joanne came up by us. She asked me to come down in the barn because one of our cows, named Fireball, couldn't stand up. This greatly surprised me. Now, Fireball was a young cow, full of energy. Normally she could jump to her feet and run to the far end of the pasture at full speed. I know if she wanted to, she could definitely outrun me. Now, here my wife was telling me Fireball won't get up, which sounded totally unbelievable.

We go in the barn and I see Fireball has her rear feet in the gutter. She tries to get up, but she just can't. I put a halter on her, and we gently pull her sideways out of the stall into the main aisle. I have done this before with cows, and almost always they will get up. Fireball tries as hard as she can. She gets two-thirds of the way up, but then goes back down. We pray for her, asking the Lord to bless her with strength to get up. I realize we better leave her alone so she can rest a while.

We go back and finish our hay and then we get at our chores. Fireball keeps trying on her own to get up, but she just can't do it. Fireball is not one to give up easily. I think I know what's wrong with her, but I call up the veterinarian to get his professional advice. He tells me exactly what I thought. Fireball has a pinched nerve so her rear legs won't work right. He says if I leave her on the concrete floor, she will never get up again. She will end up a dead cow. He tells me I need to get a 4 x 8 sheet of plywood and bolt two 2 x 6 boards on one end of it. Then I need to get Fireball on it and pull it out to the pasture. He says if I get her out on the soft grass, there's a chance she may be able to get up in time – but no guarantee. He says I may go to all that work and still lose her.

We believe in doing everything we can to save our animals. So early the next morning I go into town and buy a heavy-duty piece of plywood, along with a bunch of bolts. Joshua, Catherine and I hurry and make the sled and then carry it to the barn. We hook it up to a tractor with a log chain. Then we gently roll and work Fireball onto the sled. Then I start to pull it out of the barn and across the cemented barnyard out to the pasture.

At first Fireball didn't like it; but after she realized what we were doing, she laid on there real nice with her ears all perked up, enjoying the ride. I got her out on some nice grass, and then we got her off the sled. Being on the soft earth is a lot easier on an injured cow than concrete is. We gave her hay and water to eat and drink and kept praying for her. The other cattle came to check her out and keep her company. She kept trying to get up, but just couldn't do it. I knew as long as she kept trying, there was hope. The vet told me that if she quit trying, she was a dead cow. The same can be said for people at times. If they lose their will to live and quit trying, they end up dead too.

That night came, and we were finishing up milking, and Catherine looked out in the pasture and said, "Fireball is gone!" Sure enough, she was. Then we saw her way out in the pasture with the other cattle eating grass. She was walking real tenderly on her hind legs, but she was walking. We decided we better get her in and milk her, since it had been thirty-six hours since we had milked her last. Then we put her back out to pasture.

This is a number of weeks later now, and I am happy to report that Fireball is 100 percent back to her old self. She is back to being a very productive cow in our herd and enjoying it. We are very thankful to the Lord for answering our prayers and raising Fireball up. We look at it as a miracle. We also realize though, that Fireball had to keep trying, and that we had to do our part also. Without that sled and praying and believing, Fireball would surely have died. We must have action or work to go along with our prayers at times in order for God to answer them. We are sure glad we did for Fireball, and so is she. Now once again, she can outrun me, and most of the herd, to the other end of the pasture.

Fireball fully back to normal, enjoying life.

EIGHTEEN

Fall on the Farm

My favorite time of the year has arrived again: fall, with its many beauties and blessings. The Lord has blessed us with a great growing season this year, with plenty of rain, heat and sunshine. The Bible tells us that God gives the rain, which is God's good treasure. He has blessed us with a bountiful supply of it this year. I think we have put up the most hay on our farm this year that we ever have. It will give our cows plenty to chew on this winter. The grass in our pastures has grown fabulously for our cattle to graze on all summer long. I really like that since they harvest it themselves. It has saved me a lot of time and labor.

Now it's time to go at the corn silage harvest. We chop large chopper boxes full of super sweet corn to put into our back silo for our cattle to enjoy over the long winter months. They really look forward to this delicious treat. If for some reason, like a silo unloader breaking down, we have to skip feeding corn silage for a day, our cows look at us wondering what's wrong.

After corn silage harvest comes the high-moisture corn harvest. We hire our good neighbor with his large combine and trucks to come and harvest it. We then run the corn through a roller mill. The mill breaks the kernels up into small pieces and then blows it up into my small corn silo. Having the corn processed this way greatly helps my cattle to digest it better.

After all this comes the cornstalk bedding harvest. I take our old flail chopper out into the cornfield and chop the cornstalks back onto the field. I do this so they can dry down. A few days later, I go back out and rake them into nice large fluffy rolls. Then I go back with my flail chopper with a large chopper box hooked behind it and chop it full. Then it's off to the barn with it. I unload this cornstalk bedding onto a large elevator that takes it up into the bedding mow. Joanne, Catherine and Joshua are waiting there to take it and spread it out. It's fun and enjoyable packing away this light fluffy bedding and watching the bedding mow grow taller with each load.

Then there's the really fun and exciting part of it too. The bedding mow is next to the barn hay mow which is full from all the hay we baled this past summer. So, kids will be kids. Catherine and Joshua – along with Joanne and myself sometimes – will climb way up in the hay mow and jump down into the soft, fluffy, cornstalk bedding. We will sink into it a few feet before stopping. It is pure delight. Then it's usually back up to the top of the hay mow for another jump! I have to admit that it does help pack the cornstalks in so that we have room for more. There are many benefits to playing while you work. Even Catherine's favorite cat, Fluffy, watched us for a while one day, and then started doing it all on his own. He enjoyed it so much, he kept climbing up on the hay for another jump himself.

We use this cornstalk bedding for our cattle over the next twelve months. They really appreciate having this soft, fluffy bedding to lie on. They even like to eat a little bit of it. There's a great satisfaction in knowing we have enough feed and bedding to see our cattle through the long winter months ahead.

There is also such nice weather in the fall. With cooler days and nights comes the Master artist. The Lord paints the different species of trees in the most magnificent colors, as only He can do. Being able to view these while we work on the farm here every day is one of the side benefits of farming. But you don't have to farm to enjoy the beautiful masterpiece that God paints around you every fall. Go out for a walk or drive and take it all in. While you are doing that, thank your Creator for it all and for giving you life so you can enjoy it. We do here, for He is most certainly deserving of our gratitude.

Fluffy climbing the ladder to the hay mow.

NINETEEN

Don't Give Up

I have done a lot of trapping of animals over the years and been quite successful at it. One species of animal though, that has been hard to catch are those little furry animals that like to dig through my lawn, garden and fields. I am talking about moles. They are very ambitious, hard-working animals that just don't want to quit. They can make a real mess of a person's lawn with all the tunnels they dig and mounds of dirt they push up.

When they get in the garden, they will dig down the rows of plants, eating the roots off and sometimes half killing the plants. They don't do my hayfields any good either. So over the years, I have tried to trap them.

As a young person, I found an old plunger-type mole trap in my dad's machine shed. I just had to try it out. It turned out to be absolutely worthless for catching moles. The spring on it was so weak it would hardly put the plunger into the ground, much less kill a mole. So the old plunger-type mole trap went back into the machine shed, where it still is to this day.

I didn't give up trying though. Once in a while, I would catch a mole in a gopher trap, but that was very seldom and by accident. I remember one summer my mother was having lots of problems with moles in her garden. Now, my mother had a very large garden, and she was an excellent gardener. All the damage they were doing to her garden was very disheartening to her. Since I was the trapper in the family, I felt responsible to do something about it; so I put my brain to work on it.

I could not find any mole trap on the market that I liked. I could see problems with them all. I finally decided I would have to design and build my own mole trap. It took some doing, but out of the farm shop came a new mole trap! It turned out to be the best mole trap I had up to that point. I got rid of the moles in my mother's garden, so she was thrilled and thought I had the world's best mole trap. I caught several moles, but was disappointed with it. It took real skill to get it set just right. Then a lot of times I still didn't catch the mole. God made these little animals very intelligent. I would oftentimes have to set it several times for a particular mole before I would catch it. If I didn't give up, I would eventually catch him. I wanted a trap that I could always catch the mole with on the first setting. My trap was a long ways away from that.

Many years have passed since then. Last year I was looking at a special farm newspaper that I get. It is devoted to new ideas or inventions that people come up with. In one issue was a story and picture of a new mole trap somebody built. It looked and sounded very promising to me. I wanted to get it, but I didn't like the thirty-some-dollar price tag on it. Well, my wife Joanne and my kids strongly encouraged me to get it. They didn't really like moles either! So I bought it. This was going to be fun.

The kids and I set the trap exactly as the manufacturer told us to. We didn't catch the mole. We set it several more times and still didn't catch the mole. Now, this was very disappointing, after spending thirty-some dollars and coming up empty handed. I studied the whole situation over real good. I liked the design of the new trap better than my old mole trap, so I wasn't ready to retire the new one yet.

I made three modifications in the setting of the trap, and we were in business. In two days, we caught four moles. This was exciting. Our garden, lawn and hayfields are all doing much better also. I finally have a mole trap that I'm really pleased with. To date now I have caught seven moles with it.

Looking back on it, I am sure glad I didn't give up on mole trapping after years of disappointing results. By not giving up and being willing to change and learn, victory or success came. Since it took so long to come, it was sure sweet and rewarding when it finally did come. In life, disappointments will come, but if we will keep pressing on with the Lord's guidance, we will come out successful.

TWENTY

Your Kids Will Remember

This past summer I went out early one morning to crimp the hay in my upper hayfield next to my cow pasture. It was a beautiful morning with the sun rising in the east and a gorgeous blue sky. I always like to pray and fellowship with my Lord at this time. The birds were active, chirping and singing out praises to their Creator. The barn swallows were swooping down close to my hayfield to catch bugs and insects, then climbing back up in altitude before making another dive. They are very entertaining to watch – better than TV most of the time!

I will go out and cut hay one day; and then early on the morning of the second day, I will go out and crimp it. What is "crimping," you ask? The hay when I cut it on the first day is green, full of moisture and heavy. I usually cut it so that I leave about four inches of stubble. The fresh-cut hay lies on top of the stubble, which is good, so that the air can move through it and help to dry it, along with the sunshine. After cutting it on the first day, as it starts to dry, that force called "gravity" starts to pull it down into the stubble. By the second day, it's really down in the stubble so that the air hardly moves through it any more to dry it. This is where the hay crimper comes in. This machine, which I hook behind my tractor, has two rolls in it about six feet long. As I drive down the swath of hay, the crimper picks the hay up out of the stubble, gently crushing the stems of hay between the rolls, which helps it dry even more, and then gently lays it back on top of the stubble to finish drying. It makes a world of difference.

Then the next day I can go out, rake it up and bale it for our cattle. We get extremely high quality hay for our cattle this way. If we don't crimp our hay, it won't dry near as well. We would end up with moldy hay which the cattle don't like and which is somewhat toxic to them. On rare occasions I have seen farmers put up really tough hay that in time started on fire and ended up burning their barns down. Needless to say, I'm a firm believer in crimping hay.

On this particular morning, I had the whole field crimped, except the one last swath of hay, when it happened. I heard a bang and looked back to see that the drive shaft on the crimper had busted. It not only busted, but it got ripped up really bad. I picked up some parts and headed for home. I was thankful that I basically had the whole field crimped, but very disappointed over my machine. When I got home, I told my family I thought it was probably the end of the line for the crimper. My hay crimper is really old – about fifty years old. They quit making them about forty-five years ago. I do have a hay tedder, which is much newer, and it basically does the same job, but it just doesn't do as good of a job. Sometimes the old stuff is the best.

My son Joshua was greatly disappointed that it might be "curtains" for our old hay crimper. He kept on me over the next couple of weeks asking me if there wasn't some way we could fix it up. I told him I didn't know – we would have to see. So we made it a matter of prayer. Well, we finished haying, and I started to check into getting it fixed. As I said before, the drive line had gotten busted up really bad and needed a number of parts to fix it. I went to the implement dealership, and they were able to pull the machine up on their computer. The computer told us there were no longer any parts available for it and that the company had listed the machine as "obsolete." It wasn't looking good for our crimper, but my kids kept saying, "Isn't there some way we can fix it, Dad?"

Well, we found a couple old crimpers that had been retired, but they were different brands and the parts just would not interchange. My kids still didn't want to give up on it, so after quite a number of phone calls, we came up with a possible solution. We special-ordered some parts in through a machinery parts house and then had to take them to a blacksmith shop and get them machined just right. Also I was able to get one old part off of a junked-out crimper that my brother, Paul, had. Then it came time to put it together.

It didn't go too good with old shields, bolts, bearings and different parts from many different sources. But after many days and hours of work on it with my kids, we got it all together and working excellently, as good as new. Our kids, along with their parents, were greatly elated over it.

Afterwards when I was talking to my friend, Jeff, telling him the whole story, he made a comment which really surprised me. He said, "The biggest thing is, your kids will remember how you worked with them and had all the fun of fixing that machine up every time they see that machine in the years to come."

I replied, "I never thought about that, but I guess you're probably right." And right he is! My kids, along with myself, will remember it for years to come and take great satisfaction in it. We also will remember that God answers our prayers.

There's real satisfaction in a difficult, challenging job well done. So, parents, do challenging things with your kids. It will be good for all of you. You will all learn from it, and your kids will remember it for years to come. We are very glad we got our old hay crimper fixed, and so are our cattle. They like high-quality delicious hay to eat.

TWENTY-ONE

Thanksgiving on Our Farm

Well, it's almost Thanksgiving Day again. Once again here on the farm, we have so much to be thankful to the Lord for. He has blessed us with bountiful crops. We had the largest hay crop ever. We filled our big haylage silo the fullest we have ever had it. Then we packed our barn's haymow to the peak with baled hay, and the extra we had after that we put in our back corn silage silo.

Then corn harvest came – the biggest one we have ever had. We finished filling our back silo full of super-sweet corn silage. Then we filled our small high-moisture corn silo full of grain. We still had a lot of corn left in our field, which we were able to combine and haul to a local grain elevator to store. We will probably sell this down the road. We averaged over 170 bushels per acre, by far the best yield in our twenty years of farming here.

Then we put up the largest harvest ever of cornstalk bedding. We are so blessed and thankful to have so much excellent feed and bedding put up to see our cattle through the long, cold winter months ahead. Our cattle also have done very well this year. Our barn is full of very happy, contented, healthy cows. Our sheds also have plenty of calves in them that like to run and kick up their heels.

On the farm here we always plant a large garden every year. It helps cut the grocery bill way down, and we believe it's the best tasting, most delicious food there is. Our garden also yielded exceedingly abundantly this year.. We realize the Bible says that "the Lord gives the increase."

As we celebrate Thanksgiving this year, we will be thanking our Lord for all the blessings mentioned above. But, there's so much more than that. We are so thankful for each other. Also, we are so thankful for family and friends. It's not good going through life all by oneself. It's very dry and empty. We remember that the wonderful blessings we enjoy today came at great expense to our forefathers.

The Plymouth colonists, the first winter here, lost nearly half of their members to sickness and starvation. The next year, after a bountiful harvest, they set aside three days of feasting and giving thanks to God. They had suffered much and yet they were so grateful. Oftentimes those who suffer so much are the most thankful. They had come to this new world to escape the terrible religious persecution in their old countries. First and foremost in their lives was to serve and worship God in the way He was calling them to. There was no cost too great for them to bear in doing this. They would not mumble, complain and grumble over how hard it was. Rather, they gave thanks to God for all His great blessings.

We do the same. Life is not always easy. There are plenty of disappointments and losses in life, but we thank God for His many blessings. We are so thankful to know Him personally and walk in fellowship with Him daily. At our Thanksgiving table this year, we will once again have a large turkey with all the trimmings. We will open in prayer; and then as we eat, each one of us will say aloud the many things we are thankful for.

We all have so much to be thankful to God for. To grumble and complain at the Thanksgiving table is like poison. It is terrible. So as the old saying goes, "Count your blessings, name them one by one, and you will be amazed at what the Lord has done." From our house to yours, have a happy and blessed Thanksgiving. And remember Him who has blessed all of us so abundantly.

TWENTY-TWO

Don't be a Weasel

Many years ago when I worked on my parents' dairy farm, I used to do a lot of trapping. I started out by trapping streaked gophers for my dad for a nickel a piece. Over time, my trapping ambition grew to trapping other animals as well. Once in a while I would get a totally unexpected animal.

I well remember the summer day when I set a few gopher traps in the north line fence of the farm. I returned the next day, and to my astonishment, found I had two weasels in my traps. I had never seen a weasel before in my life, but I had heard stories from my parents about how weasels in a matter of a few nights could kill a whole flock of chickens.

A weasel is an amazing animal, measuring only eight to twelve inches in length and weighing less than a half pound. It has very thick, fine fur. It's totally brown in the summertime, except for its black-tipped tail and a little bit of white under its belly. In the wintertime, they turn pure white, except for their black-tipped tails. If it weren't for their black-tipped tails, you wouldn't even be able to see them going across the pure white snow.

It is amazing how God made these animals to adapt to their environment. When they are pure white, they are called "ermine," and their fur is extremely valuable. Since they are so small, it takes a lot of them to make a garment. Thus, only the wealthy can afford an ermine garment. Weasels have super noses, outstanding eyesight and a mouth full of razor-sharp teeth that make them excellent hunters. They kill mice, rats, gophers, squirrels, frogs, rabbits, snakes, birds and chickens.

I once heard the account of a large bald eagle that caught a small weasel and flew away with it. The eagle carried the weasel in its talons, but the weasel was not dead. As the eagle carried the weasel through the air, the weasel started chewing into one of the legs of the eagle. The eagle started to bleed very heavily and crashed to the earth and died. The weasel, which was so much smaller than the eagle, ate his fill of the eagle and then ran away unhurt. If the eagle would have killed the weasel as soon as it caught it, the eagle would have saved its life. In life, at times we would do well to finish a job, or a conversation, than to do it half way and then have it come back and bite us.

Well, I had two very live weasels in my traps. As a young kid I was fascinated by them. I thought I would be nice to them and put them next to each other. I was shocked at what happened next. They both went for each other's throat, ripping into each other, trying to kill one another. They were so enraged at being caught in their traps that they wanted to kill each other. I was amazed they were killing each other when the other one was not the source of their problem.

I pulled the two trapped weasels apart and decided I better finish them off before I or something else got hurt. I then took them home and showed them to my parents, who were greatly surprised and glad that I had caught them since my mother had a flock of chickens which she prized highly. A weasel in a chicken coop could kill a flock of chickens in a short time.

I kept trapping in the north line fence a few more days and caught one more weasel. Since that time – thirty-some years ago – I have never caught another weasel. Here, on rare occasions in past winters on my own farm, we have had an ermine. I have never seen it, but my wife and kids have. We have found the evidence of it too. We will find mice and sparrows with their heads chewed off, but the bodies totally intact. Only a weasel will do this. I do not have chickens now that I need to protect from the weasels, so I have not tried to catch them. It seems that when one does come through, it's here only a short time and then gone. Besides that, I don't want to set traps around the buildings and catch one of our good cats in them.

We all need to be careful in our lives that we don't lash out and hurt others when we are having a bad day, like the weasels that I caught. It can be very hard, or sometimes impossible, to repair the damage done. If we do hurt somebody, we can say we are sorry and ask for forgiveness and do our best to make amends, which is far more than what the weasels can do.

Twenty-Three

Christmas on Our Farm

One of the most fun and memorable aspects of Christmas for us is getting our Christmas tree. Sometimes something that starts out of necessity becomes a wonderful tradition. Years ago, right after Joanne and I were first married, we spent our first two Christmases in a trailer home. I was working as a hired man. Our finances were extremely tight so we couldn't afford to buy a Christmas tree. Those first two years we got permission from the land owner to go into his small stand of pine trees and cut one.

Shortly after our second Christmas, the Lord opened the door for us to buy our own farm. We have a good-sized woods here with a fair number of long-needled pine trees spread throughout. In the early years of our farming, finances were still tight, so the choice to go to our own woods for a Christmas tree was an easy one to make. Our young children really liked it too.

We didn't have a pickup back then, so we hooked up our old tractor to a way-older trailer and went down to the woods. We would sing "Jingle Bells" and other appropriate songs on the way down and back home, enjoying it all the way.

I have an old teddy bear that I received when I was a young child that I named "Sam." Every year Sam goes down to our woods and picks out a Christmas tree for us. He makes a trail through the woods, as only a bear can, to the perfect tree.

To get to the tree, you have to follow all his clues. What kind of clues does a bear give, you ask? Go to where we caught our last coyote. Then go to a large, hollow, raccoon tree. Then go to a badly-twisted ash tree. Then go to a large, fallen-down, pine tree and so forth. Normally he has about twenty clues for us to follow to get us to the right tree. It usually takes us about one hour to follow his trail. We have done this now many years; and even though the kids are grown, they still insist on "Sam's trail." So I still sneak out ahead of time and make "Sam's trail" for the rest of the family to follow.

The Lord has greatly blessed us over the years, as we have followed Him. We could easily go into town and buy a perfectly-shaped Christmas tree, but we don't. It's so much more special to go to our own woods and follow "Sam's trail" to our own tree. Obviously our own tree is not pruned and shaped perfectly like a purchased tree is, but it means so much more. We greatly enjoy getting it and decorating it as a family. Our focus is not on a perfect tree and perfect presents, although we sure do like our tree, and we sure appreciate the gifts we give and receive. We do all of this in recognition of the perfect gift God gave to man – His Son Jesus – to save us.

Some people feel it is wrong to put a tree up to celebrate Jesus' birth. They base this belief on Jeremiah chapter 10. In Jeremiah's day, people were cutting trees and decorating them. They were making them into idols, giving them supernatural power and worshipping them. This was idolatry and absolutely forbidden by God. We here do not make an idol of our Christmas tree. Rather, we use it to glorify God in remembering the greatest gift ever given to mankind in Jesus.

We learned a long time ago that the key to celebrating Christmas was not the perfect tree or lots of presents. Rather, it was walking in love with one another, whether we had little or much, and glorifying Christ. So this year on Christmas, as in years gone by, we will wish our cows and young stock a blessed "Merry Christmas." Then we will gather around our tree and read the gospel account of Jesus' birth and then open up our presents. We hope and pray that you who read this article also have a very blessed Christmas.

Bringing in the Christmas tree.

TWENTY-FOUR

The Rest of the Story

Over the last several months I have enjoyed writing this column. I have sought to share with others what our lives are like here on our farm. I hope and pray that these true stories have been a blessing and encouragement to many of you readers out there. I have received a number of very favorable comments from people face to face, over the phone, and through the mail. I have also had a couple of people who have been extremely upset with my writing. One yelled at me over the phone, "Not everyone believes like you do!"

The other day in town I met a real nice lady who is a very faithful reader of this column. She made a statement that totally shocked me. She said, "Tom, your stories are all so uplifting that all of us with jobs are going to want to quit them and go into farming with our families."

I was so surprised and replied, "Well, farming isn't always easy. We have problems and troubles on our farm too."

She replied, "Yes, I know, but you work together and overcome them as a family. It's wonderful!" I had to agree with her on that, but also told her there was a lot more to it than just that. Here's the rest of the story:

Shortly after I was born, my parents had me water baptized as an infant in the church they attended. We attended that church on a weekly basis; and a number of years later, I was confirmed top in my class. I remained active in the church and did very well in high school. But my life was a disaster. So much so, that at the end of 1979, I nearly ended my life. I now thank the Lord for his mercy and for good doctors. I remember waking up on January 1, 1980, in a hospital room with a TV on. The parades were on, and the announcers were talking about what an exciting, fabulous year and decade lay ahead for us. I would have liked to have taken that TV and busted it into a thousand pieces because my life ahead looked terrible to me.

Well, I got out of the hospital and went back to my old life. I graduated from high school and went to work full time on my parents' dairy farm as a hired man. I really didn't know what else to do. I enjoyed the outdoors and the farm animals, but yet my life was empty. I did not like the person that I was; yet when I would try to change, I would continually end in failure. I knew I was not right with God. I knew back then that if I were to die, or take my life, I would most certainly go to hell.

I well remember January 17, 1982. It was a Sunday, and I did not make it to church that day. It was about noon by the time I finished up all the barn chores. I stood outside the barn door looking across the landscape before me. The fields were covered with a thick blanket of snow. The trees all stood stark and leafless in the bitter cold. I stood there thinking, "Everything outside here looks so dead, cold and lifeless – like I am inside." I did not like it at all, but I didn't know how to change it.

I went into the house and started to look through a pile of stuff on my desk. I came across a book, *Meeting God at Every Turn*, by Catherine Marshall. The book really caught my attention. So I took it to my bedroom and started to read it. In the book the author tells how, as a very young girl, she repented of her sins and asked Jesus to forgive her. She made Him Lord of her life and committed to follow Him all the rest of her days.

Her account of how God so loved, guided and provided for her after this was absolutely eye opening to me. I had never heard of, or known of, a God like this before in my life. Right there, in my bedroom that day, I got down on my knees and asked God to forgive me of all the terrible sins I had committed in my life. I repented of them, and then I asked Jesus to come into my life and be my Lord and Saviour. I asked Him to lead and guide me in my life, even as He had Catherine Marshall. I promised to follow Him the rest of my life.

When I got off my knees that day, I was a different person. I knew then that if I were to die, I'd go to heaven. As I looked out over the fields and trees, they didn't look so cold, lifeless and dead any more. For the first time in my life, I was really alive.

The Bible says in 2 Corinthians 5:17 that "If any man be in Christ, he is a new creation. Old things are passed away; behold, all things are become new." That's what happened to me that day, and my life has never been the same since. He has led and guided me these many years now. Since that day I have never thought about taking my life again. I live today and do what I do because of Jesus. He has given me life and "that more abundantly." I love Him with all my heart and seek to live every day to glorify Him.

It doesn't matter where you are or how messed up your life is. God loves you just as much as he does me. He has a wonderful plan for your life, just like He had a wonderful plan for my life. I have never regretted totally surrendering my life to Him that day years ago. I just wish I would have done it sooner. If you have never given your life to the Lord, I can't urge you strongly enough to do so today.

TWENTY-FIVE

The Big Storm

Just last month in December, we got hit with a monster snow-storm here. It was a record-breaking snowstorm in that we received around twenty-four inches of snow in a twenty-four-hour period. What made it really challenging though, was the strong north winds that accompanied the snow and blew it all around.

The day before the storm hit was a beautiful, nice, calm day in which we cleaned out the young-stock sheds and gave them a nice bed of soft, fresh cornstalks to rest on. If we hadn't listened to the TV, we wouldn't have had a clue of what we were in for. When we went to bed that night, it was calm and peaceful out. We felt really good down inside because we had all of our cattle taken care of well. The TV had warned us that the storm would hit in the middle of the night, and it was right. The next morning, we awakened to several inches of snow on the ground, and the winds blowing strong.

We milked the cows and did our other early morning chores and then had breakfast. After breakfast, with a full-scale, howling blizzard going on, we all went back out to work. Blizzard or no blizzard, the cattle have to be taken care of.

Joanne and Catherine went to the barn. Joanne got the gutters ready to be cleaned while Catherine started to run feed out of the silos to feed all the cattle. Whether there's a blizzard out or not, all the cows and young stock have big appetites. Joshua and I headed for the machine shed to put the big, heavy, tractor-tire chains on the tractor that we have on the manure spreader. I knew if we didn't get them on, we would probably get our tractor and spreader stuck really bad out in the field. Even with the chains on, I wasn't sure we would make it; but I knew they would help a lot.

We got the chains on, the barn cleaned, the manure spread, and back home without getting stuck – which is saying a lot. After Joshua and I got home, he said, "It's good you drove, Dad." I had to agree with him. Then he went to help Catherine feed the cattle, and I got Big Boy out of the shed. Who is "Big Boy," you ask? That's the name we've given to our skid loader. It has been such a blessing to us over the years. I went to moving snow with him around the yard.

It took a couple hours just to open up our driveway from the blacktop road that runs in front of our building site here to the barn and house. By the time I got this done, the kids were all done running feed out of the silos. What a great blessing our children are in helping us here on the farm. We thank the Lord for them every day.

Well, we all went in for a late "noon" dinner and spent a little extra time in the house while the blizzard raged outside. Evening came, and we went out. Joanne and the kids went to milking while I started Big Boy up again and went to replowing the driveway, which took another couple hours. Our milk hauler comes in the middle of the night, so I had to have my driveway open.

I got my driveway really nice, but there was one big problem: The township still hadn't gotten the road that goes by our farm plowed. We got our chores all done and got into our nice, warm, cozy house. I said to my family that I was sure the milk hauler wouldn't be coming in the night with his big milk truck.

Catherine said she was concerned about our young stock in our upper heifer shed. The snow was drifting in so bad that she was concerned it would go over the top of the fences, and the heifers would be able to walk over the top of the fences and be gone.

So, even though it was late, dark, windy, and cold out, the kids and I took a flashlight and headed back out into the storm. Catherine was right. The snow drift in front of the building was already five feet deep. Thankfully, the cattle were all content inside the building. I didn't like the looks of it though, and decided we'd better get a gate and keep the cattle away from the big snow drift.

Getting a gate out of the back of the pole shed and up to that hill at night in a raging blizzard was quite an accomplishment for the three of us. But we did it. Having done that, we went to bed that night and slept better.

The storm ended in the night, and we woke up the next morning to a bitter-cold winter wonderland. The milkman hadn't come, but our milk tank was big enough so we could put an extra milking in it. The snow drift in front of our heifer shed was huge – eight feet deep. We started to pray that the snowplow would come through, so our milk hauler would be able to come and pick up our milk.

When mid-afternoon came, and there was still no snow plow on our road, I called up the township building and got ahold of the snowplow operator. He told me he had tried coming down our road from the north end of it that morning and got stopped about half a mile north of our place. The snow had drifted in so deep in a low area in the road that it was impossible for him to get through. He said he had called up the county for a big plow to open it up, but they said they couldn't spare one for a while. He told me though, he was loading his truck up with sand at the shop and would be over soon and try to open our road from the south. We prayed that he would be able to get through because the snow was two to three feet deep on the road going by our farm. A half hour later, a very hard-working snowplow went by our farm. Shortly thereafter, our milk hauler came. We were sure happy and thankful to see him.

Later in the week, a very large grader with a huge snowplow on the front of it, putting out a large cloud of black diesel smoke behind it, went up the road to finish opening it. We spent the next few days digging out and doing all of our regular cattle chores. It was five days before we got mail delivered to our place again.

Although the storm made a lot of extra work, by working together in harmony as a family, we made it through just fine. There is something about rising to a very challenging situation as a family and overcoming it. We have learned, as we walk in the Lord, in love with one another, we can overcome the storms of life.

Tom and Joshua putting chains on the tractor tires.

Twenty-Six

The Unnecessary Fight

Last week I went down to my woods and brought in my wildlife trail camera. Getting to the camera deep in my woods, and then back out, was very challenging with two to three feet of snow on the ground. We had had it out there for several months taking pictures of all kinds of wildlife.

Lately, with the frigid weather and the deep snow, a lot of my animal friends are gone. The bears and raccoons are taking their long winter naps. The many turkeys, along with a fair number of deer, left this area and went to nearby unharvested cornfields to overwinter at. They will help the farmers harvest their unharvested corn crop. The farmers will have a little less corn to truck out of those fields this next spring. If it weren't for those unharvested cornfields, a lot of these deer would probably starve to death by spring. With the snow so deep and hard, it's almost impossible for the deer to dig down to the ground to find acorns or old grass and alfalfa. The deer burn up a lot more energy trying to stay warm in the cold weather and going through the deep snow. I know it takes a lot of energy for me to tramp through the deep snow.

At my camera site, I started to put out about a dozen ears of corn. Sometimes though, I would put out one to two gallons of shelled corn. My animal friends really like this. By doing this,

I still had a few deer, along with several gray squirrels, and a couple red squirrels coming to visit. I also was attracting in some crows, blue jays, chickadees and woodpeckers. We are constantly amazed at the variety of wildlife that God has created.

Shortly after getting my camera home, we hooked it up to our TV to watch the pictures it had taken. Isn't modern technology great! We were watching them when all of a sudden, we came upon a very unique picture. It turns out two does came into the small corn pile at the same time. Normally does will eat together at the pile of goodies with no problem, but not these two. They went to fighting each other, standing on their hind legs, and trying to jab each other with their front legs. With their ears laid way back, they were seriously trying to hurt each other. I have gotten pictures of bucks fighting each other with their antlers, but never on their hind legs.

Although the picture was very interesting, it also was sad since there was enough corn there for both of them. If these two does would have respected each other and been willing to share, it would have went so much better for the both of them. How wonderful it is when family members walk in love and respect with one another. It makes for strong individuals and for strong families.

This is God's family plan; but how grievous it is when family members are fighting with each other and tearing one another down. It hurts everyone involved. It takes so much of the joy out of life. I have seen many of these homes, and it is so disheartening.

The Bible teaches that a good home is a little heaven on earth. I can testify from my own home here that that is most certainly true. So, commit to walk in love and respect with one another. You will be blessed. The two does most certainly would have been.

Two does fight over a small corn pile.

TWENTY-SEVEN

Tom, He Saved My Life Today

We have some good friends that we let hunt deer and turkeys in our woods every year. They enjoy getting out in our beautiful, peaceful woods. It's a chance for them to get away from the pressures of their work, and so forth, and relax in the middle of God's beautiful creation. They really enjoy being out there in the midst of all the trees with the birds and wild animals running around them. Sometimes they will have a squirrel or other animal come within a couple feet of them. It's always fun to sit perfectly still, hardly breathing, and see how close the animals or birds will come before they notice them.

Our hunters also enjoy coming to the farm here and seeing us and visiting with us. They are always interested in what is going on here on the farm. They enjoy seeing our barn cats, our dog Champ, along with our cows and young stock. A big hit for them always is seeing the newborn calves.

The big thrill though is the hunt – stalking the turkey or deer, so they can get a good shot at it and bring it home. Sometimes they're successful and sometimes not; but as my friends have said, "Whether we get something or not, it's so enjoyable just being out there." We really value that spirit because in hunting, there is no guarantee of bringing home the prized animal.

Well, two of our friends, Tim and Tom, were up one weekend

recently doing some archery hunting for the elusive white-tailed deer. They were hunting from their deer stands. Tim had a major problem though. Mr. Big Buck himself was going through the woods about 150-200 yards away from him, way too far away for archery hunting. Tim saw the solution to his problem though.

In the middle of the woods, close to where Mr. Big Buck was going through, stood a huge pine tree. It was one of our favorite trees in the whole woods. We called it "the twin towers" ever since we bought our farm here back in 1991. That was well before the Twin Towers got hit in New York City. Our giant tree had a trunk over three-and-a-half feet in diameter and stood twenty feet tall before branching in two. The two tops were eighty-five feet tall each, making the tree a whopping 105 feet tall. We always greatly enjoyed our massive, twin-towered pine tree, standing so beautiful and tall in the midst of our big woods. Then this last fall, we had a terrible windstorm here that took down a number of trees. Our large twin-towered pine tree, standing so tall, really caught the wind that day.

He looked so big and strong, like he could withstand anything, but looks can be deceiving! That day, one of his two tops broke off at the crotch and came crashing down. The top, eighty-five feet tall and over two feet in diameter, came crashing to the ground a full twenty feet away from the trunk of the tree. It came down on a large sixty-foot-tall ash tree, smashing it to the earth in bits and pieces. It was an amazing sight to behold.

Tim decided this would be a perfect place to hide since the big buck was going through just south of this. So, the next morning Tim hunkered down behind the pine tree/ash tree pile-up. Noon came, and he hadn't seen any deer yet. Tom, his hunting partner, was getting powerfully hungry and called Tim on his cell phone and insisted on going to lunch. Tim wanted to stay longer and hunt, but consented to go to town with Tom to eat. Shortly after they left, the winds really picked up strong.

Later in the afternoon, they came back and hunted till dark and then stopped at our building site to see us. Tim was real somber and somewhat shaken. We wondered what had happened. Tim said, "Tom saved my life down there today." Our jaws almost dropped to the ground in utter disbelief. We asked them what happened. Tim said, "If Tom wouldn't have wanted to go to lunch when he did, I would be dead." It turned out that while they were at lunch, the strong winds broke the other eighty-five foot tall top out of our big pine tree. When Tim got back to his site, he stood there in shock, realizing that if it hadn't been for his good friend, Tom, insisting on going for lunch, he would probably be dead. Tim said, "I'm buying Tom's dinner tonight for saving my life."

I believe there was more than Tom behind it though. We as a family, prayed to God to keep us and our hunter friends safe on our farm. We know God answers our prayers. It does most certainly pay to pray. We can't imagine living life and not praying to our loving, caring, heavenly Father.

Twenty-Eight

Old White Tail

Many years ago when I worked on my parents' dairy farm, I used to do a lot of trapping. I trapped gophers, muskrats, mink, raccoons, beavers, fox and badgers. For badgers, I had to get a special DNR permit.

Since then, I have gotten my own dairy farm, but I still enjoy doing a little bit of trapping. Although, I do not do near as much as I used to. What really makes it so much more enjoyable are my two kids along with my wife Joanne that take part in it with me. We make a great trapping team.

There weren't any coyotes around my parents' farm years ago when I trapped down there. When I bought my own farm here though, I moved into coyote country. Things haven't been the same since – for me or for the coyotes! I well remember, shortly after buying our own farm here, setting a couple of fox traps on my long field road. I was really surprised and excited one day when I checked them and found a large coyote in one of them. It was the first one I had ever caught. After that, my long field road got named "Coyote Road."

Coyotes will hunt a lot of small animals: mice, rats, woodchucks, gophers, squirrels and birds. They will also hunt larger animals like chickens, white-tailed deer and young calves. If there gets to be too many coyotes in an area, the deer herd will disappear in time, and farmers will have more calves killed by them. Thus, the reason we don't like them.

Since that first coyote years ago, I have caught many fox and coyotes off of our farm here. I am always one to watch for animal tracks on my field road and in my fields when I am out there with my tractors working. I started to get excited this past summer and early fall when, once in a while, I would see large coyote tracks on my field road. I normally wait to set traps for them until we have all of our crops in. That way, I don't have too much going on at once. We have more time to do it, and the animals' fur is fully prime and worth a lot more. We all look forward to trapping here. We find it very challenging and enjoyable to do as a family. It's also good to keep the fox and coyote populations in check.

Well, we made two fox/coyote sets in early November, along with several raccoon sets. The first morning out proved very profitable. We had a large, beautiful, gray fox and a raccoon in our traps. We thanked the Lord for them. We continued to check our traps early in the morning and caught two more gray fox, along with several raccoons. We were glad for them, but we were all looking for, and hoping to catch, Mr. Big Coyote.

About two weeks later, Joshua and I drove our pickup up to our trap sets early one morning. It was still fairly dark out, so we shined our lights on the set. We saw that we had an animal in the trap, but we were puzzled as to what it was. As we got out of the pickup, I saw that the last two to three inches of its tail were as white as snow, so I said to Joshua, "We got a red fox." A lot of red fox have white-tipped tails, but gray fox and coyotes don't.

As we got closer though, I saw that we didn't have a red fox. Its fur was more gray. So I said, "We got a gray fox with a white tail." But then the animal stood fully up, and I said, "We got a large coyote with a white-tipped tail like a red fox."

This last statement was 100 percent correct. The tip of his tail was as white as snow. I had never seen a coyote with a white tail, and I have caught quite a few over the years. I have talked to others that have had a lot of experience with coyotes, and they also say the same thing. I took him home and later that day skinned him. He measured five feet two inches long. Indeed a very large, unique coyote – a great challenge and a lot of fun to catch. We all, as a family, enjoyed getting him very much. After I had him skinned, Catherine took a picture of me holding his beautiful hide.

It is amazing how God created so many different animals and each one so special. How much more hasn't God, in His wisdom and love, created each person unique and special. When a person realizes this, it lifts their self-worth. God doesn't make mistakes. When I became aware of this, years ago, it made me love God more and want to serve Him with all my being. As I have done that, it has led to the most blessed life possible.

Tom holding Old White Tail.

TWENTY-NINE

The Big Furry Surprise

I n life we all get some unexpected surprises, sometimes good and sometimes not so good. Sometimes, when they're totally unexpected, they're enough to scare us half out of our own hides! I'm sure some of you readers out there can relate to this. This is what happened to me here a while back.

In the spring of the year, the daylight starts to get a lot longer, and the days start to get warmer. I always look forward to this time of year after a cold, snowy winter. So do others, especially the raccoons and bears that have been hibernating all winter. Spring brings renewed life, new energy and new surprises. It gets a person's blood really flowing again.

At this time of year, we are still feeding all of our cattle feed out of our silos and haymow. In my front silo, I have haylage that I run into my feed cart, filling it two-thirds full. Then, I take my feed cart into my silo room and finish filling it with super delicious corn silage from my back silo. In my back silo, I have a silo unloader that chews the feed loose with its augers and then blows it out into the silo chute. Once there, it falls to the bottom of the chute into an elevator that brings it into my silo room and dumps it into my feed cart. From there, I feed it around to a bunch of bright-eyed cows that are eagerly awaiting their treat. Normally, I feed six heaping carts to my cows every day.

It was a normal spring day here, and I was busy feeding my cows, a job I enjoy doing. I was topping my fourth feed cart off with silage when it happened. I was standing in front of the elevator, moving the incoming corn silage with my hands in my feed cart. All of a sudden, a very large, fully alive raccoon came out of the elevator into my hands. From there he jumped onto my shoulder and then onto some feed bags behind me, but not before I let out a half-scared shout! Farming can be real exciting at times.

Apparently, during the night, this coon had come out of hibernation and wandered around. Then, with daylight coming, he decided that my silo chute looked like a hollow tree and decided it would be a good place to sleep during the coming daylight hours. But by the time I was running the fourth cart out, he had other thoughts!

Well, after I let out my half-scared shout, my big brown dog Champ showed up on the scene. Now, I've never taught my dog to kill varmints; he was born with that in him! So Champ and the coon went at it. The coon would back into the corner of the silo room behind some feed bags. So Champ would go in after him, and when Champ got close, the coon would come out fighting. They would fight it out face to face, and Champ would back off some, and then the coon would retreat to his corner. After the first minute, both of their tempers were way past the boiling point! It was not safe to step in between the two to break up the fight. Just like it wouldn't have been wise for a person to step in between the US Army and the Japanese in the middle of one of their battles during World War II. A person doing so would probably have gotten killed by one side or the other! Sometimes, when a fight is raging hot, it's better to stay out of it and mind your own business.

Champ lived up to his name and after a while emerged victorious. The silo room was a terrible mess, but Champ was exceedingly happy! I had to congratulate him; he was so proud of his accomplishment.

Looking back on the incident, it sure put excitement into our lives that day. Champ was the happiest one of us all, even if he had a few cuts and scratches. I'm thankful that I didn't have the cuts and scratches that he had. The unexpected surprises that the Lord allows to come into our lives sure add zest to life at times. I've come to see in following the Lord that life doesn't get boring.

THIRTY

The Award

It is with reservations that I write this particular story; for I do not want to boast on self. I enjoy writing this column. I know there are a fair number of readers out there that enjoy reading it and that are being blessed by it. I'm very glad for that and for the feedback I've gotten from you. Of course, you like to know when something major happens in our lives. That is why I share this now.

We send our milk to a creamery that produces high quality cheese. The CEO of the creamery emphasizes that to produce award-winning cheese, it is imperative to start with exceptionally high quality milk. The creamery strongly encourages its farmers to produce the best milk possible. The cooperative is made up of about 500 member farms.

Every year the creamery gives out three beautiful plaques to honor the top three farms in the co-op. The awards are given out to the farms that produce the highest quality milk. Every time milk is picked up from a farm, a sample is taken out of the milk tank and tested for antibiotics and added water. If a sample tests positive for these, the farmer is in big trouble. The sample is also tested for bacteria and Somatic Cell Count or SCC. The lower the milk is in bacteria and SCC the better it is. It tastes better and has a longer shelf life. When this milk is processed into cheese, it will produce better tasting cheese, and the creamery will get more pounds of it for every hundred pounds of milk it processes.

The care a farmer gives his cows has a huge impact on the quality of milk that they produce. We here, seek to give our cows the very best care possible. Good cow care involves many things. Yearly vaccinations, hoof trimming, keeping the barn well ventilated and the milking equipment in excellent working order to name a few. Also, the cows need excellent quality feed to eat if they are going to put out excellent quality milk. They need a clean, comfortable area to lie down and rest on too. That's one of the reasons we put our cows out to pasture when the weather cooperates. When the bossies stay in the barn, we make sure they have plenty of good clean bedding to lie down on to relax. Also, lots of good, clean, fresh water is a necessity for these animals. All of this plays a critical role in a cows well-being.

We have always sought to give our cattle the best care possible since we bought our farm here twenty years ago. Yes, we did all this right and yet in times past we had cattle die here, and at one point we almost had to quit selling milk to the creamery. You are probably shocked at this and wonder why.

The answer is stray voltage. Stray voltage is a large, very complicated subject. When cows are exposed, to even very small amounts of electricity, the results on them are devastating. It is also very bad for people. But cows are seventy times more sensitive to it than people are.

Stray voltage over time will totally do in a cow's immune system. The result is that she has nothing left to fight disease and bad bacteria with. They will cut way back on eating and their milk will often times have extremely high levels of SCC. If the milk gets too high in SCC, it is illegal to sell it. Unfortunately, many cows go to slaughter because of this. Some cows will die right on the farm.

It has been very heartbreaking to have this happen here on our farm over the years. And yes, this happens to some degree on many dairy farms today. Stray voltage is invisible and hard to detect, unless one is checking for it.

Where does stray voltage come from, you ask? It can come from a number of sources. One is the power company can send it in on their neutral line. That happened here once years ago, and we lost a number of cows from it.

It can come from old wiring and electrical boxes in the barn that leak a tiny amount of current out. We've had that here too, and lost some of our beautiful cows from it. And what a lot of people don't realize is that it can come right in through the earth. Some of the electricity used in homes, businesses and on farms goes back to the power plants through the earth! If a path of this electricity goes through a farmer's barn, the end result of this is going to be terrible!! We've had to deal with this here too over the years.

A number of times, when we've had stray voltage problems here, we were not able to get anybody to help us solve it. Sometimes, the power company would just deny it existed or walk away and say it was our problem. After losing cows a number of times and not being able to get anybody in here to solve the problem, we seriously started to consider whether we should sell our farm and buy another one. We prayed about it, but we didn't have a peace in our spirits about it.

I had a good basic understanding of electricity and how it works. But, these stray voltage problems were monsters. One big problem with stray voltage is you can get it solved and things will go good for a while, but then it will come back in some other way. We've had this happen here many times over the years.

During one long trying incident when we couldn't get anybody to solve the problem here, we earnestly sought the Lord for wisdom and guidance in what we should do. Then, one sunny summer afternoon when Joanne went to town, I decided that I should go in the barn and look in the main electrical box and try to figure it out. It is recommended that farmers not do this because of the electrical dangers involved with this! But, I felt in my spirit that I should do this, and so I did.

That was the start of one long, vast, learning experience for us here. For all that I've learned on this subject, I could easily write a big long book on it. But, I most certainly am not planning on doing that.

After spending much time in prayer and working on the electrical system here, we have gotten our farm really good. We give God the glory for it, for without Him and His wisdom, we would not have been able to do it. That is a fact.

We diligently seek to take the best care of our cows that we can. Part of that care is checking our barn daily for stray voltage. We know that our cows are a gift from God, and we are thankful for them. We realize that we are stewards over them and that someday we will give an accounting for how well we cared for them.

Recently, our creamery had their annual meeting. We took second place of all the farms in the creamery for the year. After all the challenges here over the years, it means a lot to us to receive this honor. We are not personally competing against other farmers, but rather we work alongside them to produce high quality food to feed a hungry world.

It was a great honor to receive this plaque and recognition. Previously, we had received the 3rd place award three different years from the creamery. We give God all the glory and honor for them. For without His blessings and wisdom, we would not be farming here today!

The creamery's representative presenting Tom and Joanne their award.

THIRTY-ONE

Our Own Farm – An Answer to Prayer

April is a special time of year for us on our farm. We bought this farm in March and moved on to it in April of 1991. It was a huge step of faith and a brand new beginning for us.

After our daughter Catherine was born, it became very obvious that there was not a future for us on my parents' dairy farm. Joanne would pray daily as she went about her house work and taking care of our new young baby. I would pray while I worked on the farm, and after the evening chores were all done, I would walk out into the fields praying to the Lord. And then together, we would earnestly seek the Lord as to what He had for us. Over time, He spoke to both of us individually that He had a farm for us.

Starting in January of 1991, I started going to auctions and buying old, used machinery. We had to start to borrow money to pay for it too. And yet we didn't even have a farm, much less any money. But we had faith in God; we took Him at His word that He had a farm for us.

We also started to look at farms for sale. We knew with just the two of us to do the work, we couldn't get too big of a farm. Also, with extremely limited finances, we couldn't afford much. We knew that any farm that we bought, we would have to get a land contract from the owner. In a land contract, we would pay the owner of the farm a set amount every month for a number of years, until we got it paid off, or until we could refinance through a bank.

We looked at many farms, and finally found a really nice one. We had a peace in our spirits about it. We met with the farmer several times, setting a price for the farm and for some of the personal property on it. We also discussed and agreed upon all the legal language and responsibilities in the land contract. We were so happy and thankful to be getting our own farm! It was a dream come true.

Sometimes dreams crash and bust all apart. Sometimes when it happens we have no idea why it happened. This is what happened to us. We were due to go to the attorney's office in just a few days and sign all the paper work and make the down payment on the farm.

I came home late one night from milking cows on my folks' farm and just got into the house when the phone rang. The farmer told me he couldn't sell me his farm. He was going through a real nasty divorce, and the lawyers told him that he couldn't sell the farm until the divorce was all settled. They informed him that it would probably take a year or two to settle it.

I talked to him a while and told him how sorry I was to hear it. I hung up the phone and told my wife the news. We then bowed our heads and prayed for him. We then looked at each other and said, "We know God has a farm for us, if it isn't that one, then it's a different one."

So I kept going to auctions and buying old machinery, and we kept looking for a farm to buy. We eventually found a farm to buy that had been rented out for several years. We sold our mobile home and the acre of land that it sat on to make the down payment on our farm. It's the one we call "home" today.

After many years here, and many trials, struggles, improvements and accomplishments, this farm to some degree has become part of us. It is the farm that the Lord had for us. Every spring, we look back and remember how God miraculously guided and provided for us. God has been faithful to His word in giving us a farm of our own. We are so thankful to Him for it.

If we would not have earnestly sought the Lord in prayer, I'm sure we would not be here today. Almost everyone that we talked to back then strongly advised us not to get our own farm. They said we would go bankrupt; there was no way we could make it. Other farmers were selling out left and right back then, a number of them having gone bankrupt. But, we knew, after much prayer, what God had said to us. So we went ahead in faith and never looked back. God has most certainly been true to His word.

It has been and is so wonderful having our own farm. God has been so good to us. I often say here, "we walk under an open heaven." That is most certainly true.

If you are at a very difficult place in your life, I can't urge you strongly enough to earnestly seek the Lord. He is loving and has a wonderful plan for your life – I know from personal experience.

What about the farmer that couldn't sell his farm to us because of the divorce? He called me back a long time afterwards and thanked me from the bottom of his heart. He told me that during the time period that we were dealing on his farm, he was contemplating suicide. He said the only thing that kept him going was the love he had seen in me and my wife. I was shocked at that statement, for I had no idea he was in that condition. Even though we did not get his farm, I'm sure glad the Lord brought us together, so that we could be a blessing to him.

THIRTY-TWO

Bless Your Wife

May is a very special month of the year for us up here in the "north country." Summer has finally arrived and the wonderful planting season has come again. As a farmer, I enjoy putting seeds into the ground, and seeing new life come forth. With the miracle of new life coming forth, comes the promise of another harvest.

May is also very special for two other reasons: one is Mother's Day, and the second is my wife's birthday. The Lord has blessed me with a wonderful wife. I could never have hoped for a better one. Joanne has been a very godly mother and wife over these many years.

So when May comes around every year, I try to do something special to bless her. Sometimes I may take her out to dinner or buy her some flowers. That is fine and she greatly appreciates it. But, I'm the more practical type of guy too. I like to do something that will not only bless her on her special day, but continue to bless her many days down the road.

So, I'm always keeping my eyes open for some way to do that. A number of years ago, I came up with a great idea.

On the north end of our barn, we have a big sliding door that opens so that we can put the cows out on the barnyard and out to pasture. In the summer time, we like to leave that door open, so fresh air can move through the barn. The doorway frame was originally built so a heavy pipe gate fit into the frame. That way, if a cow got loose in the barn on her own, she couldn't run out to pasture.

The pipe gate was made of heavy two-and-one-half-inch pipe. It was super strong and super heavy. It needed to be because once in a great while, a big cow or heifer would get riled up and jump over the gate. Usually when the cow was half way over the gate, she would have roughly a thousand pounds of weight on it. That big old heavy gate never bent though.

There was one problem with it, however. Because of the weight, it was difficult for Joanne and the kids to take it on and off. They never ever complained about it, but I could see it would be wonderful if I could do something to change it. I really liked how the builders had designed it; I just didn't like the weight. So over time, I gave it a lot of thought and came up with what I thought was a good idea.

I knew two-inch-diameter, stainless steel pipe that is used in milking systems is extremely strong. Being it is only one-sixteenth inch in thickness, it is very light. I told the kids what I was thinking and told them I wanted to do it as a surprise for their mom and give it to her in May. I asked them if they wanted to help me with it. They were eager to do so. They had one big question though, "Would the stainless steel gate be strong enough to support a big heavy cow without getting crushed to pieces?"

I said, "I don't know, but I think so. There's one way to find out and that is to build it and use it. If a cow goes over it in the future, we will know the answer to your question for sure."

We always had to wait for Joanne to leave the farm before we could start to work on it. I also had to get some material on the side without Joanne knowing about it. We eagerly worked on it every chance we got. It didn't go as easily as we had planned, but in the end we had a beautiful piece of work to be proud of. It weighed about 15 percent of what the old one did.

Well, on the special day, we gave it to Joanne. The kids and I were excited to give it to her. She was totally surprised, almost speechless when she saw it. She never had a clue what we had been up to. It was so much lighter and easier for all of us to handle. Over the years, she has been very thankful for it and has always remembered how her loving family blessed her one special May. We all like it; it's a gift that keeps on giving. That's usually the best kind in my opinion.

Yes, since then one big heifer did go over the top of it. It sprung it a tiny bit. We had to do a little bit of work on it to get it back perfect. So it has stood up all these years and been a blessing. Every time Joanne takes the gate on and off, she remembers that she is greatly loved by her family.

I'm glad we could bless Joanne in a very practical way. She sure liked it, although I also know that she likes flowers or something else special with it too. Husbands, on Mother's day, or your wife's birthday, do something special for your wife. Show her that you love her. In doing so you will bless her and fulfill the Scripture in Ephesians 5:25 that says, "Husbands, love your wives." Give of yourself to her, and you will both be blessed.

THIRTY-THREE

Lark – Our Indian Cow

Years ago, I remember seeing a John Wayne movie called *Angel and the Bad Man*. John Wayne was the bad man getting in trouble with the law. The excellent, old wise sheriff was keeping a close eye on John, waiting to catch him breaking the law. He figured it would be just a matter of time before he would be stringing John up by a rope. The justice system worked a lot faster back then, than what it does today.

The wise old sheriff would keep sneaking up on Wayne's back side totally unexpected. He and his horse would be standing right behind John, without John knowing it. John wanted to know how he could sneak up so quietly with his horse and not be detected. The sheriff explained that he had been an Indian fighter and had trained his horse to be perfectly quiet. It was his Indian horse.

The movie ended well in John Wayne giving up his outlaw ways and marrying a beautiful Christian woman. Together they became farmers. It's so good when a movie has a good ending.

I tell you all this to tell you I have an Indian cow named Lark. No, I didn't get her from the Indians, but she's just as quiet and sneaky as the sheriff's horse. She is a pest and has a mind of her own, but we love her.

Lark is a big 1,500-pound dairy cow that is super friendly. When God created Lark, He put a lot of creativity into one cow.

Every spring, the kids and I go around all the fences to make sure they're in good shape. We usually end up driving in some staples and splicing broken wires. We usually end up using a heavy mall to drive fence posts back into the ground that the frost heaved out the previous winter. This kind of work gets a person in real good shape!

In the movie, John had to deal with the Indian pony. Here, I have to deal with my Indian cow which is far worse. We will be out fencing, and there will not be a cow or anybody else in sight. We will be working on the fence, minding our own business, fully absorbed in our work, and then it will happen.

I will get a gentle bump from behind that will make me take a step forward. It half scares me out of my hide so to speak. It's the last thing in the world I'm expecting when I'm busy working on the fence. And of course, it's Lark. Who else could it be?

She sneaks up behind us; we never hear her coming, and she gives me a good gentle bump on my back with her nose. Then when I turn around and look at her and say, "Lark, you Indian cow," she'll stand there, real bright-eyed, ears all perked up and shake her head at me in such a way as to say, "I got you again." And she's gotten me many times that way. She wouldn't do it to the kids if I'm there; it's always me. She has it out for me. The kids think it's great and we all end up having a good laugh over it.

But, it doesn't end there. In the barn she's a regular pest at times. If one of us is up in front of the cows feeding them, and we have our back towards Lark, watch out! She will grab our shirt in her mouth and half pull it off of us. Or literally half rip it off of us. If she can't do that, she will give us a big lick with her big tongue. We always quickly turn around to see it's

Lark. Who else could it be? And she's got that big, bright-eyed, mischievous look on her face that says, "I got you again."

Lark is one of my best cows and super friendly. Although, the sheriff's horse was super disciplined, which Lark most certainly is not, I would not trade Lark for the horse any day of the year. Lark is a real pet and friend. As I said earlier, God was real creative when He created her. I'm glad He gave her to us here. We sure enjoy her, even if she rips our shirts half off at times.

I know too that God is real creative in every person that He creates. He gives everyone special talents and abilities. If God creates such a special cow, how much more doesn't He create you special? He loves people far more than He loves cows. I have come to see this over the years as I have followed Him.

Lark bumping Tom in the back.

THIRTY-FOUR

Memorial Day

As a young child growing up, I never knew what Memorial Day really was. I knew a lot of people got long weekends off to go to the lake or to do whatever else they wanted. But for me, it was just another work day on my parents' dairy farm.

That all changed one summer day when I was helping my uncle George on his dairy farm. George was a very hardworking dairy farmer who had never gotten married. So he greatly appreciated it when I could come and help him during the summer months. He had a 240-acre dairy farm with beautiful rolling crop land and three different woods on it.

I would help George all day long on the farm with his work. We got along great. Then at night, I would sleep in one of the upstairs bedrooms in his old farmhouse. The one I always chose to sleep in had one window that faced to the east. I really liked that because I woke up to the rising sunshine each morning.

The bedroom was not fancy at all, but it didn't have to be. It only had one picture in it hanging on the south wall. The picture really intrigued me. It was a way-old picture, about four by six inches in size. It showed five or six strong young men dressed up in their best clothes. I had no idea who they were at all.

On one particular day, George sent me to rake a hayfield that was next to the woods on the northwestern corner of the farm. I had never been in those woods in my life. The woods started out on level land, but it had a steep hill in the middle of it. As I was raking hay next to it that day, I wondered what was up in the woods. It was extremely heavily wooded and had not been logged off in decades.

Well, curiosity got the best of me that day. I decided to stop the tractor and take a few minutes and go exploring. I started climbing the steep hill and got up it a ways when I came upon something that shocked me. There in front of me was a large hole in the hill. That was the last thing I expected to find.

I studied the hole; I could see a large amount of shale rock had been quarried out in the past. But I was really puzzled by it since there was no road or trail leading away from it. The whole area around it was grown up in large trees. I didn't have a clue who had done it, or when, or how they had gotten the rock away from there. I knew that I would have to ask my uncle George some questions that night when we would milk the cows together.

I quickly headed back out of the woods and finished raking the hayfield. We got the hay all baled off that day, and evening milking came. I was really looking forward to that evening so I could ask George the big questions that had been on my mind all day.

I told George how I had found the big hole up in the woods that day. Then I asked him my questions concerning it. He had all the answers to my questions. I am so thankful these many years later that George would talk to me and answer my questions, whatever they were. I learned a lot from him. Now as a parent these many years later, I try to answer all the questions my kids put to me. Although, I must admit I can't answer them all, but I do my best. I know we as parents are to instruct our children in the way that they are to go. If we do it right, the Bible promises us that when they are old, they will not depart from it.

George told me that when he was a child about my age, he went exploring in that woods one summer day also and found the big hole. So he asked his dad about it. His dad, which would be my grandfather on my mother's side, was born in 1888. His family bought the farm in the early 1890's and went to work clearing the land and building buildings.

George asked me if I had ever noticed the old picture in my bedroom, to which I replied, "Yes." Those men were all part of the family living and working on the farm at that time. In 1897, they quarried the rock out of the hill in the woods to build one of the buildings on the farm. It was hard work, using dynamite, picks and horses, but they enjoyed it. By the end of that year, they had a beautiful building to show for it. There is something very satisfying in working hard and seeing the fruit of your labor afterwards.

It can be catching. Over the winter months, they were so pleased with their new building, that they decided to build another one the next summer. It would mean quarrying a lot more rock, but they were excited and up to the task.

But then something happened that stopped their plans dead. On February 15, 1898, the battleship USS Maine was sunk in Havana harbor. The United States went to war with Spain. Our government called for volunteers to go to war and fight. Three of the young men in my bedroom picture answered the call. They went and never came back home. They died on the battlefield. The new building that they had dreamed of building also died on the battlefield. The big hole in the woods was never touched again.

Milking cows with George that evening, I came to realize how so many Americans before me had dreams and so much living that they wanted to do, and yet they laid down their lives on the battlefield so that we could be free and live out our dreams. That night Memorial Day took on a whole new meaning for me. I thank the Lord for those who have laid down their lives for us, and I also pray and thank the Lord for those serving our country today.

Freedom and liberty are not cheap; they have cost a lot of blood, so let us live our lives wisely. If we live our lives wisely, in the end we will be thankful; if we don't, we will be sorry.

Three of the young men in my bedroom picture who went to war.

THIRTY-FIVE

The Tractor Joanne Bought

Y ears ago, when we started farming here, I bought an old 1206 Farmall tractor on an auction over in Minnesota. It's been my big tractor on this farm here for many years. Built in 1966 by International Harvester, it was one of the best tractors ever produced. Up until a few years ago, I did all my plowing and chopping with it.

I used it a lot, but with age, it started to have a number of breakdowns. Though not major, they would stop me from using him until I got it fixed. When a farmer has crops to get in, he can't be waiting around for parts to fix his tractor. I did not have another big tractor as a back-up. I was blessed though, to have a couple of very good neighbors who lent me one of their big tractors on a couple different occasions when I desperately needed one. We thank the Lord for good neighbors.

A few years ago, after our 1206 had yet another breakdown, we decided to look for another tractor to take his place. We most certainly were not going to get rid of him; we had plenty of other work for him to do. We appreciated our neighbor's generosity, but it isn't good to depend on that too much!

So, after praying about it, the decision was made to find an excellent used tractor, one that we could afford. We started to look through all the local papers that listed tractors for sale.

We also talked to our neighbors and local implement dealers concerning one. We came up with a lot of good leads.

We were on a mission to find an excellent tractor. We all had "red-tractor fever." About the only thing that will cure "red-tractor fever" is a nice red tractor!

I would call the owner of a tractor that I would find for sale and ask him a lot of questions about it. He would assure me that his tractor was an excellent one. From our phone call, we were sure we had found the right one. So we would go and look at it with our check book in hand and be totally shocked at what we saw. The tractor that he told me about over the phone and the one we would look at would often times be total opposites!

This happened continually; it was starting to get depressing. Our lawn needed cutting, machinery needed fixing, and we were running all around looking at tractors and coming home disappointed.

Finally, I called a dealer a ways away that I knew in the past had gotten old tractors in. He would buy good old tractors cheap, and then in the winter time when things were slow in his shop, he would have his mechanics rip the tractors down and go through them, fixing whatever needed it. Then they would give it a new paint job and put it out on their lot for sale.

The dealer, Roger, told me by doing this he could keep his mechanics on over the long winter months, instead of laying them off. He said he only broke even on it financially. I must say though, that I think it was really decent of him to do. I like to see people staying employed doing productive work.

Roger informed me that he had a tractor in the shop almost done that he had gotten from Nebraska. So once again, with the lawn needing cutting, we drove out of the yard here to go and look at another tractor. This time we were not disappointed. We found an excellent used tractor. I test ran it, and it was perfect.

The only problem was the price was more than what we were planning on spending.

We told Roger that we would talk it over and get back to him on it. Joanne wanted to buy it, but I was hesitant on it. The price was a fair bit more than what I had planned on spending. I told Joanne that with all the farm expenses that we already had for the year, we didn't need this big one. She realized that, but said we really needed the tractor. I had to agree with that. And the price was just 10 percent of what a new one that size would cost.

Well, I called Roger up and told him that we'd take the tractor. A couple of weeks later, he delivered a bright red 1466 International tractor to our farm. Joanne got right out there with the checkbook in hand and wrote the check out! It's the first tractor she ever bought. I must say that she has excellent judgment! Then, right after that she gave it to me for a Father's Day present. Wow! What a gift.

It has proved to be an excellent tractor here over the years. I'm glad I let Joanne buy it. I've learned over the years to listen to my wife. She has a lot of wisdom and insight. She has been a great blessing to me.

Husbands, love your wives and consider what they say, and you will be blessed. I know I am every day. I really know it every time I look at my big red tractor!

Tom standing by the tractor Joanne bought.

THIRTY-SIX

Enjoying Our Work

I knew for the last several months that we had a tough job coming up here on the farm. The job ended up being harder than what I expected, but also more enjoyable. I know to most people that would sound like a contradiction but such was the case.

In my silos here, I have silo unloaders that save us a lot of work by getting the feed out of the silos for us. They have two augers with sharp little knives on, which go around on top of the feed chewing it loose. Once the augers have the feed chewed loose, they feed it into a blower that shoots it out of the silo into the silo chute. From there, the feed falls down into an elevator which brings it into the barn to a waiting feed cart. Once we have the cart full, we feed it around to a bunch of bright-eyed cows waiting for lunch.

Now, my silo unloader is fourteen years old, and the blower was getting in bad shape from all the feed it had blown out over the years. Unfortunately, in this life things do wear out. Sometimes, when I have a lot of things wearing out at once, I like to think of heaven, my future home, where things never wear out.

The silo unloader dealer told me he was sure he could rebuild it and save me a fair bit of money over buying a new blower.

That sounded good to me, but I had my doubts on whether it was in good enough condition to rebuild.

I decided that my daughter Catherine and I would take the silo unloader apart and take the blower to the dealer's place where he would rebuild it. Then later we would go and get it and put it back into the silo unloader. In doing all this ourselves, we would save a lot of money, not having to pay the dealer for two trips plus a bunch of labor. I know many farmers would hire the dealer to do all of this, but we try to do all that we can to save money and be profitable here.

We got all the feed run out of the silo early that day and then went to taking the unloader apart. It turned into quite a job with all the big old rusty bolts that needed to come out to free the blower from the unloader. The first few bolts came easy, which we were thankful for. The rest of the bolts were a different story though.

On one bolt, I was using a breaker bar with a socket, putting all the muscle I had into it, while Catherine held the other end with a wrench. All of a sudden there was a loud bang, and my socket went flying. We were both surprised at that. I picked up my trusty old socket to find it had busted! So I sent Catherine to the shop to get me another socket that size. Well, with using sockets and wrenches, hammers and cold chisels, hacksaw and electric hand grinder we got all the bolts out. We then used a gear puller to get the pulley of the blower shaft. We finally had the blower free of the unloader. It had been far more difficult and time consuming than what we had expected, but we got it.

We got the blower out of the silo and looked it over good. We both thought it looked unfixable. We loaded it on the back of the pickup and took it out to the dealer's place. Since he was gone, we left it there for him. Two hours later, he called me up and told me a new one was $1020. In other words, the old one was junk! He told me that he had to get going, but he would set a new one out for me.

It was cow milking time, so I didn't want to take Catherine or Joshua with me to get the new blower. The blower weighs well over a hundred pounds and is clumsy to handle, so I needed somebody to help me.

I was blessed though, in that the answer had arrived just an hour before. Two friends of ours had come and were planning on hunting turkeys the next morning. I explained to them that I could use help getting the blower and that I really could use their help getting it up into the silo. They were more than willing to help us.

We drove out to the dealer's place and found the blower and new bolts that he had laid out for us. As I was looking over the stuff there, my two friends grabbed the new blower and started to carry it to the pickup. I thought, "Boy, this is real service," and I was thankful for it because I was pretty wore out from the hard work up in the silo that day.

We got back home and got the blower out by the silo chute. I had Catherine get into the silo, and I got into the silo chute. Our two friends were standing on the ground looking things over, and one said to the other, "Yea, now I'm beginning to see what Tom's been talking about concerning needing help." Then the two of them lifted it about six feet up into the silo chute to me, and then I worked it in through a door to Catherine. With it being way late, we called it quits for the night and thanked our two friends for helping us so much. They said that they were more than glad to help us. It is such a blessing of the Lord to have good friends.

Early the next morning, Catherine and I went to work putting the unloader all back together. We got it done by noon. As we were carrying a lot of the tools back to the shop, Catherine said to me, "Dad, I really enjoyed doing that project. I like doing projects."

When she said that, I thought, "Wow, what a wonderful daughter I have."

She then went to running feed out of that silo for the cows again. She reported back to me later that the silo unloader was running much better than what it had before. I told her that we must have done something right then!

Even though it had been much more difficult than we had anticipated, we worked super well together. We got a tough job done and enjoyed working together on it. It is so rewarding to me to have my family help me here on the farm and be blessed in it.

Parents, you need to play and work with your children. You can teach them so much in it. You will be blessed more than you realize, and they will be also.

THIRTY-SEVEN

America – A Land of Dreams and Equality

Often times as I work on my farm here, I think of what my ancestors went through to come to America. I think of my great-great grandfather, August Ferdinand Heck, and his wife, Wilhelmine, with three young children making the decision to leave Germany and sail for America. August was forty years old, and Wilhelmine was almost thirty – not exactly young kids!

The timing of their leaving Germany and coming to America truly amazes me. Mid-March 1861, they set sail for their new home country with their youngest child being only six weeks old. A country starting to go into a terrible bloody civil war. I think I would think twice before going to a new country if that country was going into a civil war that could destroy itself.

But they came, arriving seven to nine weeks later, stepping ashore at Baltimore, Maryland, in the month of May. A month later found them half ways across the country in La Crosse, Wisconsin. There, for the next three years, he worked as a tenant farmer. Then, in 1864, they moved by ox team and wagon, sixty-five miles north to Canton Township in Buffalo County, Wisconsin.

There, they homesteaded eighty acres and bought an additional forty acres on which they built a log home for their family. Over the years his family grew and so did his farm. They ended up having fifteen children, and the farm grew to 280 acres. Needless to say, August and Wilhelmine were very hardworking Americans. And they loved America dearly. It was their home, their country.

But, under all these circumstances, why did they come to America, you ask? August told his descendants a number of times over the years why he came to America. His answer shocks most Americans today. His answer: "Because he was tired of bowing and paying homage every time the King or a Prince went by in the street." He wanted to bow to only one, to God the Father and His Son Jesus.

The Founding Fathers of this country believed the same way. They believed that all men were created equal by God. It is so sad that they didn't fully put into practice what they put in the founding documents of this nation. It would have saved so much suffering, death and destruction which the Civil War brought.

Fortunately, this country survived the war, and freedom came to all people here. In America here, people could pursue their God-given dreams and live in freedom like no other people in the world.

I know America has had many shortcomings and faults, and still does, but like August Heck, I believe it's the greatest country in the world to live in. In America here, we don't have to bow to any man or woman. We have the privilege though, of bowing to our Creator and Saviour. August did, and so do I. He is the only one worth bowing to.

THIRTY-EIGHT

Kangkleberry Pie

Many years ago, shortly after we moved to our own farm here, we would go down to our big woods with our small children. Usually it would be a Sunday afternoon in the middle of the summer. We would go there to pick wild berries to put into a pie. There weren't many down there, but we could always find enough red raspberries, blackcaps and blackberries for a super-delicious pie.

The sweetest berries in the world are the wild ones. They are not the biggest ones, but they are most certainly the best ones. Maybe that's why they are the hardest ones to get too. Sometimes the things that are the hardest in life turn out to be the most rewarding. We really had to work to get them. All the brush, canes and thorns made it very difficult to get these highly prized berries. We would each take an empty ice cream pail and go after them though.

Sometimes there would be surprises waiting for us in the brush, such as squirrels, chipmunks and other small animals. Also, the pretty berry-eating birds would be in there. Robins, blackbirds, blue jays, catbirds and so forth. They all know good eating when they see it too. The Creator made all of these animals and birds very intelligent. It was fun to see them all and very educational for the kids.

On one occasion, I got a very scary, totally unexpected surprise. I was picking some really big juicy blackberries off of a bush that was growing around a tree that was about fifteen inches in diameter. The tree had a real smooth one-inch diameter hole in it about four feet up from the ground on the front side of it.

I really didn't think anything of it. Mistake number one!!! I had gotten to the place where I had most of the plump berries picked off of this bush. But there were still a few nice ones to get on the back side of the tree. So, I set my pail on the ground right next to the tree, so I could reach further to get those super delicious berries. Mistake number two!!!

While I was reaching around the tree, the hole in the tree came alive! Hundreds of enraged honeybees came flying out of that hole, just like you see on a Tom and Jerry cartoon. Only in this case, it wasn't funny. Well, I think I moved as fast that day as any US Marine does in boot camp! Maybe that explains how I managed to get out of there without getting stung.

There was one big problem though. My pail, with a lot of berries in, was still sitting by the tree. The bees, which were extremely upset, were swarming around the tree. I decided the best thing to do was go and help somebody else pick berries and come back later for my pail.

When it got time to go home, I went to retrieve my pail. The problem was the bees still hadn't settled down yet. The problem was solved though, by getting a long, lightweight tree branch that was laying on the ground a short ways away. By sticking the branch real slowly and carefully in the handle of the berry pail, we were able to retrieve it safely. Needless to say, I never picked berries by that tree again.

We would take the highly prized berries home and Joanne would make a pie out of them. I told my kids that years ago my teddy bear Sam would pick all kinds of wild berries and make super delicious pies out of them. They were the best pies in the whole world. Since they were a mix of different wild berries, Sam came up with a unique name for the pie – kangkleberry pie. How he came up with that name, I really don't know, but it stuck. The kids thought it was great; they were having the same kind of pies that Sam had had years earlier.

Then, as we milked cows that evening, we would all be eagerly looking forward to the warm, fresh-baked kangkleberry pie waiting for us in the house. When we got our chores all done, we would sit down and give the Lord thanks for the pie and the good day He had given us. We would then eat it along with a large glass of cold milk. It was absolutely delicious! I'm sure no king ever ate finer. Sometimes, when we had extra berries, we would freeze them and then have a pie in the winter time.

We have found it is wonderful doing things, even simple things together as a family. God has put all of us into families to bless us. By doing things together as a family, you will all be blessed. I know we are. We sure like our kangkleberry pie.

THIRTY-NINE

Small Things – Big Problems

We had a very puzzling situation happen here on our farm early this summer. It took us a while to figure out what was really happening. We had a cow, Lydia, get lame on one of her legs. So we lifted her leg up so that we could look at her hoof. Just like people's toe nails need trimming once in a while, so do cow's feet (or hooves). We trimmed her hoof a little, but it actually looked really good. So we were puzzled as to why she was so lame on that leg. A few days later though, her ankle swelled up really big. Somehow she had sprained it quite severely. At the time, all we could figure out was that she must have misstepped and hurt it. But we had no idea how.

Very shortly thereafter, one of our biggest cows came into the barn with a hurt leg. Again, we lifted up her leg and looked at her hoof. It was perfectly fine. Within a few days, her leg swelled up too. Over the next several weeks, we had a few more cows get sprained ankles or swollen up legs. We were baffled by this and greatly concerned about it.

We made this a matter of prayer. We prayed for healing for our cows and for wisdom in what to do about this. We kept talking it over as a family, trying to figure out exactly what was happening to cause our cows to get so many injuries. One thing started to come to our mind.

We have a cemented barnyard for our cows to go out onto before they go to pasture. We have a feeder wagon there with feed on for them along with a large water tank for them to drink out of. Part of it had been cemented many years ago by previous owners of this farm. They had over time poured in many small slabs of concrete. Over time, with freezing and thawing and normal wear and tear, the edges of the different slabs started to wear down and separate some. We knew there were a couple of small pot holes out there where a few of the slab's corners came together.

We finally came to the conclusion that our cows were hurting their legs by stepping into these two small pot holes. Well, I decided to fix them fast. I called up a local contractor and asked him what kind of cement mix to use to patch them with. Then the next day, Joanne and Joshua went out there and started to clean the cement off real good while Catherine and I got our cement business ready.

When we were ready to start to mix up a batch, we went out on the yard to see exactly how much we would need. We were shocked at what we saw. Joanne and Joshua had done an excellent job cleaning the old concrete all off. There weren't just a couple of pot holes; there were several of them. Not only that, but some of the slabs' edges had worn a lot over the years and with the freezing and thawing had gotten one- to three-inch gaps between them. We now fully realized why we had so many cows with leg injuries.

We also realized that a small patching job was not going to fix this problem. I went right to the telephone and called up my contractor friend. I told him what I found and that I figured we would have to bust out all the old concrete and pour in one large hunk of new concrete. He agreed with my conclusion. Then I told him that we needed it done really soon. I was not going to let my cows out there and risk any more injuries.

Glen said he could squeeze us in – in a couple of days. I thanked him and we went back to work. We put away our cement patching stuff. We then proceeded to move our feeder wagon along with our big water tank off the yard.

The big day came, Glen and his crew showed up a little after 7 a.m. They came to work with a jackhammer, mall, concrete saw and other tools. I was ready with the skid loader and a large dump box. We got the old concrete all busted out, loaded and hauled away. Then, we had a big cement truck bring in a large load of redi-mix cement. We got it poured that same day, for which we were very thankful.

After that, we let it harden a few days, and then we put our feeder wagon and water tank back on it. Then, we let our cows back on it, and by their behavior we could tell that they really appreciated it. It was so nice!

That was a month ago now and I am happy to say that we have not had any more cows with leg injuries. If I would have realized sooner how bad that old concrete was out there and how the cows were hurting their legs on it, I would have replaced it long ago.

Unfortunately, we did lose one cow from this. Most of the cows are healing up well though, for which we thank the Lord. He most certainly does answer our prayers.

In life small things can cause big problems, just like the small holes and cracks in our concrete did. Things like drugs, alcohol, cigarettes, bad habits and so forth can destroy lives, families and relationships. They can start out so innocent looking, but over time can become really bad – just like my old concrete – and do great damage.

I know from my own life that has been true. But when I have changed, I and those around me have been blessed. Sometimes, I've had to call on the Lord to help me, and He has. If you will call upon Him, He will help you too.

FORTY

A Good Neighbor

We always chop our first crop hay and put it into the silo as haylage. The cattle really like it this way and we can get it put up a lot faster than if we were to bale it all. By getting it put up faster, we get better quality feed for our cows and second crop can start to regrow sooner.

A while back, I was out chopping first crop hay. We had worked hard at it, and this was our last day of it. We were all looking forward to getting done. I had about five loads left to chop when it happened. I turned the spout on my chopper way to the side to finish filling the chopper box full. The spout turns with a hydraulic cylinder. One end of the cylinder is attached to the spout. The other end is attached to the blower of the chopper along with a heavy channel iron to support it. I tried turning the spout back, but it didn't go!

I stopped chopping and got off the tractor and went back and looked at it. The heavy channel iron had busted in two, and the two plates attaching the cylinder to the blower had busted loose from the blower and gotten bent up really bad. Needless to say, when I saw this, I let out a groan and said, "Oh no." I got back on my tractor and headed back home to the shop with it.

Joanne, Joshua and Catherine came right away when they saw me pull up to the shop with it. I am so blessed to have such a wonderful family that is eager to help me here on the farm whenever I need help. They are a real blessing of the Lord in my life every day.

I could see that this was going to be a major fix-it job. And I knew I didn't have time for it then. I told them that I just wanted to straighten the spout, so I could finish chopping the last few loads. We disconnected the cylinder and tried to straighten the spout by pushing on it with an oak plank. We couldn't budge it. We decided to get our skid loader and push on the bottom of the spout with it while the kids pushed on the top of it. It took all we had even then, but we finally got it straight. I then headed back to the field with it and finished chopping that day. We were so glad to finish it up with the chopper in the condition it was!

I knew that I had to get my chopper fixed before second crop hay. The bottom of the spout fits over the top of the blower by about seven inches. The manufacturer only put one grease zerk in it to lubricate it. On later models they put four zerks in because of all the problems they had with their earlier models. Needless to say, almost all their earlier models had busted apart like mine just had.

I called a salvage yard and found that they had a lot of choppers like mine. They only had one though, that hadn't busted up like mine had. Catherine and I headed to the salvage yard and got the channel iron brace along with two steel plates that we desperately needed.

I knew I would need another man with more tools than what I had to help me fix our chopper. I knew who that was – my good friend and neighbor, Howard. I called him up and told him what the situation was. He was more than willing to help us. We have worked very well together over the years helping each other. Good neighbors are a great blessing from the Lord.

So, on the appointed day, I took the chopper up to his place.

He knew all about it since a number of years before, his chopper had broken up the same way. It came apart terribly hard. Once we had it apart, Howard went to welding on it while I went to grinding and putting in more grease zerks so that it wouldn't happen again. We thought we could get it fixed in a few hours' time. Sometimes, our figuring is way wrong though. It took us seven hours to get it fixed.

But, get it fixed we did and better than new! Since then we have used it on second crop hay and it has worked excellently. Thank the Lord.

It is wonderful when neighbors walk in love and harmony with each other, helping each other out in times of need. The Bible teaches we are to love our neighbors and bless them. In doing so, they will be blessed and so will we.

Tom chopping hay with the chopper his neighbor helped him fix.

FORTY-ONE

A Big 20 by 60 Miracle – Part 1

Many years ago when we bought this farm, it had two small silos on it. The smallest one we used for storing high moisture corn in for the cows. The other one we used to store haylage and corn silage in. Since that silo didn't hold a lot of forage, we ended up baling about 10,000 bales of hay a year to feed to our cattle.

I would go out and bale a wagon load full of thirty-pound alfalfa hay bales and then bring them in and unload them onto an elevator. The elevator would take them up into the haymow where Joanne would be waiting for them. She would start to pile them away. When I got done unloading the wagon, I would hurry up into the mow and help her finish piling away the bales. Then I would hurry back to the field for another load. We really had to work hard and keep moving to get enough hay baled up over the summer months to last our cows through the long winter months ahead.

Handling all those hay bales in the hot hay mow was a lot of hard work. We never complained about it though, we were so thankful to the Lord for the farm He had given us. We couldn't afford to hire somebody to help us to do it either. So, Joanne started to do something secretly in the haymow that even I didn't know about. She started to pray over and over again thanking the Lord for all the beautiful hay and asking Him, "Lord, isn't there some way to make this easier for us?"

When a righteous man or woman prays in faith to the Lord, they can expect an answer – even if God has to do it in the most unusual ways!

It was late in the summer of 1992, and we decided on one nice Sunday afternoon to drive down and see Joanne's uncle John on his dairy farm. Uncle John was always super nice and friendly; we always got along great with him. On this particular day, John had something he just had to show me. He had just gotten a used silo put up to store corn silage in. It looked beautiful.

Needless to say, John and I were both impressed with it. I was already starting to get ideas for our own farm. John told us that the silo had come off of a farm a couple miles down the road where the owners had quit milking cows. Thus, they had no need of it anymore. John had some Amish farmers just down the road from his place that he had helped some in the past and had become good friends with. They offered to take the silo down and put it back up on his farm for a set price. John agreed and ended up with a very nice silo.

On the way home from John's that day, we were busy talking about our time with Uncle John, and I said to Joanne, "If I could get a silo for the price John did, I would sure consider putting one up for hay."

Joanne just lit right up and said to me, "You would?"

To which I replied, "I certainly would."

She came right back with, "Will you pray about it?" I gave her my word that I would. She was all smiles and very happy. As I said before, I didn't know that she had been praying about this for quite some time already.

I knew of a business just a few miles away from my farm that took down and rebuilt used silos, so on Monday morning I gave them a call. I told them the size of silo I was wanting and he gave me a price estimate. His price about floored me. It was about double what John had paid. I then realized that John's Amish neighbors had done it for him largely out of friendship. We farmed fifty miles away from John, and we obviously didn't know his neighbors. So it was becoming apparent to me that it was financially impossible for us to put up a silo.

With the heavy debt load we were carrying, I had no idea how we could come up with the money for a used silo. I came to the conclusion that a silo would have to wait a number of years until we could pay our debt down a bunch. But, I had given Joanne my word that I would pray about it. I didn't see what good it would do since I was sure the answer was, "No."

I know God expects a person to always keep their word, so one night after we were done with our evening barn chores, I went out on the hill behind our barn to pray. I prayed to the Lord saying, "Father, I don't see any way that we can put a silo up here with our finances being what they are, but I told Joanne that I would pray about it, so that's what I'm doing. What is your will in this?"

The Lord spoke loud and clear to my spirit, "You can have it if you want it."

I stood there in shock at His answer for a few seconds and then replied, "Lord, I want it; You're going to have to provide the means for it though." Right after praying that, I had a peace in my spirit that He would do it. I had no idea whatsoever how He would do it, I just knew He would.

I didn't tell anybody what the Lord told me that night – I knew it was best to keep my mouth shut and let the Lord work. I knew in my spirit that if I tried to work it out, I would end up making a mess. I knew to totally leave this in the Lord's hands.

The Lord moved real fast. A couple of days later as I was working around the buildings, an older man driving a pickup drove into my yard. I walked up to the gentleman and greeted him, wondering what he wanted.

The miracle silo.

FORTY-TWO

A Big 20 by 60 Miracle – Part 2

The Lord moved real fast. A couple of days later as I was working around the buildings, an older man driving a pickup drove into my yard. I walked up to the gentleman and greeted him, wondering what he wanted. He stood there for about a minute looking around my farm yard and then said to me, "Is there something that you could really use on the farm here?"

To which I cautiously replied, "Yes."

He then asked me what it was and I told him a silo to chop our hay into so that we wouldn't have to bale so much. He stood there thinking for a minute and then said, "I'm no farmer, but I can see that would be good."

He went on and said, "I'll loan you X amount of money, interest free, and you can repay me a set amount every month till you get me paid in full. Will you take the money?" This sounded too good to be true, yet I knew from past experience that the Lord at times will work that way. I hesitated, wondering if there was some catch. Lots of times if something sounds too good to be true it is. Many people have gotten hurt on deals that were, "Too good to be true."

He saw my hesitation and asked, "What's wrong?"

To which I replied, "What's in this for you?"

He said, "I just want to help out a young farm family."

I didn't know what to say, since I didn't want to get caught in some trap. So I finally said, "I can pay you some interest on the money you loan me."

To which he replied, "I don't want any interest."

I stood there stalling not knowing whether to accept it or decline because this was looking way too good to be true. He finally said to me, "Why won't you take it?"

To which I replied, "Why do you want to do this? What is in this for you?"

To which he replied, "I live in town and I have neighbors around me that are able to work, but won't. They stay up till two to three o'clock every night, playing their loud music and drinking beer. They go to the local food pantries and get all their groceries. They are perfectly healthy and can work, but they refuse to do so. They collect all the assistance they can and make life miserable for their neighbors. So when I see a young family out here working so hard trying to make it, can you give me one single reason why I shouldn't be able to help them?" By this time he had tears running down his cheeks.

To which I replied, "No, I can't."

He said then, "You'll take the money then?"

To which I said, "Yes."

"Good," he replied, "I'll bring you a check next week." True to his word, the next week he showed up with the check.

The check was not enough to buy a silo, but I figured if we saved all we could over the coming winter months, we could put up a silo the following spring for haylage. We would also need a silo unloader, and new ones were very expensive. I told Joanne that I wanted to put up a big enough silo so that down the road we wouldn't need to put up another silo for hay. I figured a silo twenty feet in diameter and sixty feet tall would be perfect for the number of cattle that we had. To get a silo this size would take all the money I could scrape together. I said to Joanne that I wanted to do it right the first time because if we didn't, it would cost us a lot more down the road. She agreed.

Her question, "What about a silo unloader?"

To which I replied, "We're putting all the money into the silo so that we get a big enough one, let me figure out the silo unloader business." That satisfied her.

I went to a local salvage yard that had junked-out silo unloaders in it. They were there because they were worn out. I told the owner of the salvage yard that I needed a silo unloader for a silo I was putting up. He frowned at me, but said that I could look through his junkyard. Most of the stuff there was totally junk. I could see this wasn't going to be easy, but I wanted this silo, so I was pursuing this dream with all that I had. Often times the really good things in life require a lot of us, but in the end they are worth it.

I found two old junked-out silo unloaders that had been made by the same company and figured I could take parts from the two of them and make one workable unloader out of them. The junkyard owner sold them to me very cheaply and offered to deliver them to my farm.

These two silo unloaders were a long ways from being able to run, but over the next several months I worked on ripping them apart and making one workable unloader out of them. It was a tremendous challenge, but I enjoyed it.

Spring came and with it a silo-building crew. It was wonderful to see the big silo actually going up. Once completed, I went to work assembling my silo unloader in the silo. The man who loaned me the money showed up the day I finished the unloader and test ran it. It ran really well.

The expression on his face was priceless! He said, "I never thought you would ever get that old piece of junk to run again.

I thought you were crazy even trying, but it wasn't my place to tell you so!"

I replied, "I never doubted that I'd get it to run again."

To which he responded, "I know, but I didn't have the heart to set you straight. I just can't believe that thing is running!"

And run it did. I had to keep fixing on the thing over time, but it did bring the haylage out of the silo for us. I ran that unloader for four years; then it got to the place where it was absolutely beyond fixability. But, by then we had got to the place where we could afford a brand new silo unloader.

What a blessing that silo has been. It has made haying here over the years to go so much faster and easier. It has resulted in getting higher quality hay put up for the cattle. The cattle really like it better too. As a result, they eat more hay and make more milk. That was a benefit that I hadn't counted on. As a result, we got more money in our milk checks that helped pay off the loan on the silo.

So, Joanne got her secret prayers answered that she prayed in the hay mow. God answered them in a most unusual way. I am so thankful that she prayed and that I kept my word to her and prayed also. Once again we learned not to limit God in answering prayer, even if the situation looks almost hopeless. With God there is always hope. With Him there is always a way. That's one reason we love Him so.

FORTY-THREE

Baby – A Special Little Calf

Sometimes things don't happen as they should. That's true in life for all of us at times. And it is most certainly true in dairy farming.

A while back, we were all anticipating our cow, Blackie, calving here. Blackie is all black, except for a little white under her belly and some white on her ankles or stockings as some people would say. Blackie is one of our older cows here, and this would be her fourth calving.

Exactly five weeks before she was due, Joanne noticed her acting differently one morning. We kept an eye on her throughout the day, and it became very obvious that she was going to calve.

By mid-afternoon, she still hadn't calved, so I decided to examine her. She was in labor, bringing forth a calf. I was sure though that the calf was dead. Not at all uncommon for a calf being born five weeks early.

Later that afternoon she brought forth a way-small heifer calf – about half the size of a normal, newborn calf. Boy were we surprised though! The calf was alive. My diagnosis of it being dead was totally wrong, and that is one time I'm glad that I was wrong. When we touched it, we startled it, and it let out a loud beller. Furthermore, it was a beautiful red and white calf.

Since it was born so early, it couldn't stand on its feet to get milk from its mother. So, we carried it to a nicely bedded pen. Then we proceeded to milk Blackie. The newborn wouldn't drink milk, so Joanne took a meat baster and slowly squeezed milk into its mouth. Slowly, she swallowed it. Joanne and Catherine are super at taking care of special needs animals on the farm here, for which I am extremely thankful.

We name every newborn calf on our farm. Since this one was so tiny, we named her "Baby." Since Baby was born so early, we knew it would be an uphill battle for her to make it. We prayed, thanking the Lord that Baby was born alive, and we asked Him to bless Baby to grow and do well.

We learned from past experience to give calves that are born so early raw chicken eggs along with their mother's milk. Every day, for the first few weeks of Baby's life, she received two to three eggs daily.

Blackie and Baby have both done very well over the last few weeks. Baby now drinks out of a pail all by herself and enjoys running around with the other calves. She even moos at us to let us know when she's hungry!

Two days after Baby was born, another cow, Olive, calved. She gave birth on time with a beautiful calf. We named her calf "Oliver." It is amazing the difference in size between Baby and Oliver. They are real pen pals.

Even though things did not work out exactly as we would have liked them to, with the Lord's blessings they did work out. In life things come to us in ways we don't like at times. With the Lord's help though, we are able to rise above them and glorify Him. In doing so, we are blessed. We are sure blessed to have Baby today. She is sure blessed to be here too.

So the next time when things aren't working out the best for you, don't grumble and complain, rather, turn to the Lord in prayer and trust Him. That's what we do here. It makes for a much better and rewarding life. Baby is proof of that!

FORTY-FOUR

The Chief's Tree

Many years ago, as a young person, I would sometimes stay with my uncle George helping him out on his dairy farm. Usually this would be in the summer time, but once in a while I would help him in the fall, and one year I even spent Christmas vacation helping him.

He lived with his mother and pretty much ran the dairy farm all by himself. Thus, he greatly appreciated my help and company when I was able to stay with him. I would help him take care of the cattle and put up the crops. By doing this, I got to know him and his 240-acre farm quite well.

George was a very hard worker that took great pride in keeping his farm up. He had a beautiful farm with gentle rolling land, except one corner of it towards the far back end. That had some very steep, hilly land on it. Some of that was fenced off in two different hunks of pasture, and some of it made up two different hayfields.

After working there over a number of years, I came to notice something very mysterious back in those steep hills. Between the two hayfields ran a fence line that was part of the fence line for the two pastures on the sides of them. In this fence line, between the two hayfields where the cattle couldn't get at it, was a very strange tree growing.

I have never seen another tree like this before or since in my life time. It stood four to six feet tall and stayed green year round. It never grew taller than that, and it was the only tree in that whole fence line. It was kind of brushy, and I didn't have a clue what kind of tree it was. There wasn't another tree like that in the whole area either.

I came to realize this after raking one of the two hayfields back there one summer day. After I realized this, I decided I would have to ask George about this when we milked cows together that evening. Milking cows with him was a great time to talk and learn from him. Children need time to talk to and to learn from adult family members. Adults need to take time and listen to their children and teach them what they know.

Well, we got the hay baled up from that field that day, and evening milking came. Once we had the milking units on the first cows, I asked George about the strange tree on the back end of the farm. His answer shocked me, and as we talked it over, I came to have a great respect for that tree.

Here's the story behind the mysterious tree: George's grand-parents, which would have been my great grandparents, bought the farm in the early 1890s. His grandparents, parents and even he himself cleared a lot of the land of trees and stumps. When they cleared the land back there, they also noticed this very unique little tree. Since they also had never seen a tree like this before, they decided to leave it and put the fence line next to it, thereby protecting it and saving it.

In time some Indians passed through the area who were familiar with that particular tree, and they told my great grand-father about it. The tree is planted on a little hill towards the upper end of a valley. When you look to the north, you have a beautiful valley opening up before your eyes.

The Indians said, "Years ago, it was a tradition when one of their chiefs was getting close to dying, he would pick his burial site. Then, when he died, his tribe would bury him there and plant this special tree on top of his grave to honor him. Only great chiefs could have this tree planted over them."

Where the Indians got this special tree from, I have no idea. My ancestors though, always had a special respect for that tree and that site. After milking cows with George that evening, I also had a special respect for it.

But, that is not the whole story behind that tree. George informed me that that tree would grow up to be four to six feet tall. It would live for many years and then die and become a bunch of dead brush. Then after a couple of years, it would start to grow back from the roots again.

For the tree to die, and then grow back, and then die again would take forty to fifty years. He said his family had witnessed this tree do it two or three times over the many years they had had the farm. This tree grew, lived for many years, and then died. But then it lived again. The Indians believed too, that their great chief would live again.

God, the Creator of us all, has put that truth in our hearts. Since this is true, we all need to live wisely, remembering that we will answer to God someday for how we have lived our lives. Although I have not always lived wisely, I am so thankful for Jesus, my personal redeemer and friend. With Him at my side, I can stand before God blameless. I hope the old Indian chief knew my friend Jesus also.

FORTY-FIVE

Don Nelson – A Veteran Who Made a Big Difference

In this life, I have had the privilege of meeting a few very remarkable and honorable people. Such people have a lasting influence on other people's lives. The man on top of my list is Don Nelson.

Don grew up as just a regular city boy in Minnesota. Then World War II came along and everything changed. Don got the job of being a ball-turret gunner aboard a B-17 Flying Fortress flying over Europe during 1944.

Don was looking forward to coming home soon. He had 23 bombing missions completed. When a crew got to 25 they got to come home. Mission number 24, on August 6, 1944, took them to Berlin and the most concentrated anti-aircraft weapons on earth.

Right over Berlin, his Flying Fortress got blasted right out of the formation and fell into a deadly flat-spin. A fire raged in the bomb bay as the plane raced toward the ground. Don, along with some of the others, parachuted out. Within five seconds of Don jumping out, the plane exploded.

Landing in Berlin, Don was marched by gunpoint to an army post. A German captain greeted Don by literally busting his nose. The blood poured from his nose. He couldn't get any medical attention for it either. His nose would bother him the rest of his life. Why did the captain do it, you ask? The day before the captain's wife and children were killed in a direct bomb hit.

Don was put in a prisoner of war camp with many others. It was an absolutely terrible ordeal. Many of the men were killed, and others starved to death. The treatment was brutal. I will not say anymore on that except to say as he was telling me about it, the tears were just flowing down his face. By far, the majority of prisoners in his camp never saw the end of the war. Don did though.

What happened after this is one of the saddest parts of the story. Don would wish for the rest of his life that he could undo it, but he couldn't. After he got freed, he, along with a friend of his, got rifles and went around the streets of Berlin putting the guns to people's heads and robbing them. He told me, "We wouldn't have hesitated at all to have pulled the trigger and killed them if they would have refused." Don and his friend got a great deal of wealth doing this. They reasoned that for as terrible as they had been treated by the German soldiers, they had the right to do this. We must always be careful that we don't justify doing wrong just because we were wronged. That doesn't make it right.

One day when they had a gun put to a man's head, an American army officer came up on them. He put a stop to it immediately. Don and Augie reported to a US company of soldiers right away.

Later on he returned home and was discharged. He was never tried for his war crimes. But, it was a terrible weight he would carry for the rest of his life.

Don was finally back in Minneapolis with his wife, Gen. Once home, the bar life called out to Don and his friends. They would stay to closing many nights. On one unusual night, Don did not go out drinking with his pals. That night one of his friends got killed in a car accident.

Three days later, Don, with his drinking buddies, were sitting in the front row of the church as pallbearers. The funeral sermon struck Don as a big joke. The preacher said, "This fine young man was baptized in this church as an infant. His name was inscribed upon the Cradle Roll. He attended the Sunday school and received promotions. He established formal membership in this church at the age of eighteen. He has contributed, from time to time, to the work of our missions. The hope of victory over death is strong…"

After the sermon, the pallbearers headed to the cemetery and started to laugh and joke about it, that is all but Don. One of the men said, "It sounded to me like we really got him off to a good start."

Another one said, "When that preacher got to going on about what a great guy he was, I wanted to look in the casket and see if he's the same guy I knew." The men then all roared with laughter, that is all except Don.

The men noticed Don was totally quiet and asked him what was wrong. Don replied, "Just thinking, if that sermon was as big a whitewash as I think it was, then he isn't going to heaven. And if he isn't, neither am I."

With the funeral over, Don returned to his drunken ways. It wasn't long after that, that Don ended up in a car accident. And to top that off, his wonderful wife Gen was about ready to take their young daughter and leave him. Don didn't like it, but he seemed powerless to do anything about it. Sin can so entrap a man, that he is powerless to change.

One thing did change in Don's life though. His good drinking buddy, Joe, didn't show up for a few weeks. Then one day, Joe was at Don's door all excited. Joe said, "I tell you, Don, this

LIFE ON THE FAMILY FARM

is the most important thing there is. The Lord has made me a new person. I've been born again."

Don was drinking a beer and replied, "What you've probably done is blown a fuse in your skull."

Joe answered, "No, this is reality." Joe pleaded with Don to accept Christ as his Lord and Saviour, or end up in hell.

Don's response, "Lots of good company there, all of my best friends."

But Joe wouldn't give up; two weeks later he took Don and Gen to a good gospel preaching church. The preacher preached a powerful salvation message and at the end walked down the aisle where Don was seated and said, "Jesus has paid the price for your salvation. Will you take the gift He's paid for?"

Don's heart was just pounding in his chest as the pastor spoke directly to him. "What about you, young man? Are you going to stop with 'almost persuaded' when you can say 'yes' to Christ?"

Don mumbled back, "Don't I have to do something to be saved?"

The pastor replied, "What could you possibly do? Can you find all the people you've wronged and make it right?"

Don thought back to all the people in the city of Berlin that he had robbed at gun point and slowly shook his head. He replied, "No, sir, and I can think of a lot of them."

The loving pastor then said, "But Jesus has paid the price for every sin. Your redemption has been paid for in full. Now take it and become a child of God. Take it and find out what God has for you in your new life." Don did. Don repented of his sins and asked Jesus to be his Lord and Saviour.

A few days later, Gen said to Don, "I don't understand you. Last week you were a devil, this week you're an angel."

Don's reply, "It's the Lord."

A few days after that, Gen, while she was washing dishes, also received Christ into her heart and life.

And yes, God did have a whole new life for them. He called them to Alaska in 1956 to be missionaries in small remote villages. They had no running water, no electricity, but they were thrilled to be in God's family and preaching Christ to others.

In time they built a radio and TV station at North Pole, Alaska. The call letters are KJNP, which stand for King Jesus North Pole. Their signals go out to several nations on the top side of the world.

Don entered heaven on May 8, 1997. After Don got saved, his whole heart's desire was to live for Jesus every day and to tell others about Him. I have never seen a man so consumed with the love of God and the desire to serve Him as he was. Don would do anything for Jesus.

I have counted it as one of the great privileges in my life to have known Don. I still think of him often, and someday I will once again talk to him on the other side.

He was a veteran who made a lot of mistakes, even as I have, but by God's grace and turning to Him, his life, like mine, was totally changed. To God be the glory.

FORTY-SIX

Grandpa, He Followed His Heart – Not the Money

My grandfather, Paul K. Heck, was born in Buffalo County, Wisconsin, in 1898. He was the eleventh of thirteen children born to Ludwig and Constance Heck.

On the early pioneer farms back then, lots of children came in real handy to help with all the work. Breaking land of all the trees and stumps, rocks and roots, took a lot of work. Then, planting the crops and tending them, along with taking care of the livestock and household needs, added up to a considerable amount of work. Thus a big family was a real blessing.

When the children got to be adults, they would often times strike out on their own and find their place in the world. Often times this would mean marriage and starting a family of their own on a new farm.

But, as I visited with my grandfather late one night after milking the cows on my parents' dairy farm, he told me his life didn't quite go that way, which surprised me. I had always assumed it had. Parents and grandparents, you need to teach your children and grandchildren the things you know. The world out there will teach them a lot of wrong things. Teaching your kids the right things will help guide them in their lives.

Grandpa told me when he was in his early twenties, his folks really didn't need him on their farm anymore. He had some relatives that were pioneering a farm out in Washington State that invited him to come out and help them. So in early December, Grandpa got on a train and headed west. It was quite a trip for somebody who had never been away from home before in his life.

He settled down and helped his relatives with land-breaking for six months. Grandpa was a very strong, hardworking young man. Men like him could always find work. And there was plenty of work available in that area, especially in the lumber industry.

The lumber industry was booming, so Grandpa headed for it. There was a large sawmill close by that was hiring. The sawmill was located in a building on a large mill pond. The pond was filled with logs that had been floated down the river with the spring melt. Most of the trees were the giant redwood trees that grew in that part of the country. Grandpa's job, with the help of a number of other men, was to get the logs up to the sawmill building. It was hard work, and somewhat dangerous, maneuvering the logs on the water, but he enjoyed it.

One day, they had a big challenge. The opening on the sawmill building was eleven feet square. They had an exceptionally large log though, that was thirteen feet in diameter! A log that size had a lot of lumber in it. The question was: "How do we get it into the building to get it sawed up?" Grandpa had an idea. He proposed taking a large crosscut saw and sawing the butt of the log down to just under eleven feet square. It would be a lot of work, but he was sure they could do it.

The sawmill operator didn't like the sounds of that though. He proposed ripping the front of the building out to get the giant log in. Since the sawmill operator was the owner, his idea won. They ripped the building wide open and got the log to the saw. Afterwards, they spent the rest of the day fixing the building back up. They had a lot of beautiful lumber to show for it and a great sense of accomplishment in a job well done. But, sixty-some years later as Grandpa told me this, he still thought his idea was the best one!

Grandpa then said, "The money out there was outrageous. Way too much. You couldn't begin to make that kind of money back here in Wisconsin." He went on to tell me that he worked there six months and then returned to Wisconsin by train. He said, "I got back in early December, so I was gone exactly one year."

I was surprised by all of this and said, "If you could make such outstanding money out there, why did you come back to Wisconsin?"

I have never forgotten his answer in all of these years. "I had my eyes on a pretty young girl back here before I left. I came back for her." That pretty young girl was Ottelia Roetter whom he married in April of 1923. They ended up farming here in Wisconsin, raising a family and being married sixty-four years.

Grandpa followed his heart, not the money, and was greatly blessed because of it. He never regretted coming back to Wisconsin. I remember after Grandma died, how greatly he missed her. Oftentimes, I had seen Grandpa living his life to bless others.

It is sad to see in this world today so many people living totally for self. Because of it, we have so many divorces, broken homes and wrecked lives. I know from experience that the truly blessed life is one that follows God and His ways.

FORTY-SEVEN

The Totally Unexpected

Sometimes people can be going through life with everything going normal, and then totally unexpectedly they get hit with something that knocks them flat on the ground. That something can come in the form of many different things, but one thing for sure is that it is not wanted or welcome, yet we are forced to deal with it. How we deal with it will determine what the outcome will be. Often times it radically changes our lives.

That is what happened here on December 13, 1992. It was early on a Sunday morning. We were expecting a child to be born to us in April of the coming year. But that morning, Joanne was not feeling well and felt she better get in and see the doctor. The doctor confirmed what we felt down inside – the baby was on the way!

This came as a total shock to us. We had been praying and standing on a lot of different Bible verses in the preceding months that this pregnancy would go full term without any complications. Now the doctor confirmed that the baby was coming. He did a quick ultrasound and, judging by the size of the child's head, decided the baby was 24 weeks old. He quickly contacted Minneapolis Children's Hospital, which was one of the leading hospitals in the nation for babies born prematurely. They said the youngest age they would take a "preemie" at was 24 weeks.

We were believing God for life, and we believed that every life is precious. We made the decision to go for it. They told us that there was barely a 50 percent chance of the baby living. But, since we know and serve a God that answers our prayers, we were not without hope.

They got Joanne on a helicopter and flew her to Minneapolis, landing on top of the hospital. Very shortly thereafter, our son was born. They put him in the NICU, Newborn Intensive Care Unit. They quickly confirmed that he was not 24 weeks old, but only 22 ½ weeks old! It turned out that he had a larger than normal head which he inherited from his dad who also has a larger than normal head. If they would have known from the original ultrasound that he was only 22 ½ weeks old, they would not have taken him.

While all of this was happening to Joanne, I was home on the farm here milking the cows and doing all the other winter chores. Dairy cows do not give a farmer time off. Nevertheless, Joanne and I did stay in close touch over the phone. It was very hard being separated from her, but I had no choice.

Worse than that, I was here the next couple of days doing my chores in a daze. I really didn't know what to think or hardly how to pray since things had not gone the way we had been praying. And then one morning it happened. As I was stepping in between two cows to milk them, the Lord spoke to me as loud and clear as I've ever been spoken to in my life. He said, "If you believe Me, he'll live. If you don't, he won't."

I replied, "Lord, I have no other choice then, but to believe you for life." And that settled it for me. I stood on His personal Word and on the Scriptures every day and never doubted once. I was like a large bull dog with a meaty, juicy bone. I was not going to give it up, period. I realized afterwards that since we had been standing in faith for our son for months already, I already had a strong foundation built to stand on.

The day came when I went over to Minneapolis to get Joanne home and to see my new son. We already had named him Joshua, the name the Lord gave us for him. For before he was ever conceived, the Lord told us we would have a son and that we were to call him "Joshua." It is so interesting that the name *Joshua* means "The Lord saves." In this case, only the Lord could save our Joshua. But for Him to do so, we had to believe Him and walk in faith.

Once I arrived at the hospital, I quickly embraced Joanne and kissed her. Then we were immediately taken in to an office where a psychologist and the head doctor of the NICU confronted us. The psychologist told us how terrible it was that our world had totally fallen apart.

My reply was, "My world hasn't fallen apart at all, we are believing God, and our son is going to live!"

She tried to get me to face her "reality," but since I kept standing on the Word of God, she finally quit, looking at me as if I was some kind of nut. I didn't care what she thought. I knew what God had said and I wouldn't give one inch on it.

Next, Dr. Hoekstra informed us that any child born before 24 weeks of age had a very slim chance of living. I told him that Joshua was going to live. He then went on to tell us all the complications that result when a child is born so early. My response was that we would pray and believe God to bring him through each one of them. He went on to tell us that if he were to live his chances of being a normal, healthy boy were very slim.

I said, "He will live and be a healthy boy."

The doctor informed us that it would be a long road. I will have to say he was very nice. By the time he got done talking to us, the psychologist looked like she thought I needed to be locked up! It is a sad situation to see people who don't know God and live hopeless lives.

Joshua was one pound and ten ounces when he was born

and shortly after that dropped down to one pound and seven ounces. We kept praying and standing on the Word of God daily. We kept seeing miracle after miracle. Joshua spent his first few months in the hospital, and then the big glorious day came when he came home. Since then, Joshua has grown and become a strong, healthy young man. We give God all the glory.

It's interesting that several weeks after Joshua was home here, Dr. Hoekstra called me up on the phone one day and said, "I don't understand it. There were some days when I left the hospital that I knew the next time I came back that Joshua wouldn't be alive anymore. But, every time I came back he always was alive for some reason." I knew the reason why. God is always true to His Word. If He can find people who will stand in faith on His Word, He will do it.

Even when we get hit with the totally unexpected, with God there is always hope and a way out. God has not yet run out of miracles for His children.

Joshua today with his puppy.

FORTY-EIGHT

My Valentine

I remember back many years ago to a very special time in my life, February 14, 1989. It was Valentine's Day, and it was the third month that I had been dating a very beautiful, godly lady named Joanne.

Even though neither one of us were rich financially, we felt that we should splurge that day and make it really special. It was special to me already because this was the first time in my life that I had a girlfriend on Valentine's Day. I bought Joanne a large heart-shaped box of premium chocolates ahead of time to give to her.

I did the regular farm work that day and then milked the cows that evening in great anticipation of seeing my sweetheart. I dressed up super nice and then drove the thirty-some miles to pick up my valentine. When she came to the door, I was stunned. She was absolutely beautiful.

Even though that was twenty-three years ago, I remember it as though it were yesterday. She was wearing a beautiful cream-colored dress, with cream-colored heels and a sharp red scarf around her neck. After exchanging some greetings and giving her the box of delicious chocolates, we went out to eat at a fine restaurant. Since I had milked cows that evening, it put us pretty late, and thus the place was virtually empty. We had it all to ourselves except for the cooks and waiters. It looked like I had bought the place out for my special date!

We ordered our special meal, and when it arrived, we thanked the Lord for it. We asked Him to bless it and our time together. The lights were turned down way low as we started to eat and visit. We then noticed a short ways away that somebody had earlier that evening ordered candles for their table. Since the people were long gone, and the candles were still burning, I brought them to our table. We dined like a king and queen that evening. I still remember as if it were yesterday, looking into Joanne's radiant face that evening in the flickering candlelight. I've come to realize that God is the author of romance.

We visited long that evening, and then I took her home. Then it happened. Before I left to go home for the night, we kissed each other for the first time. Wow!

I am happy to say that we kept our relationship pure before God and man. Several months later in August, I had the privilege of marrying my valentine, my soul mate.

Every year on Valentine's Day, we think back to our first one and celebrate anew the love God has given us for each other. We also let our children know that they are special to us.

So this year I will be getting my valentine a big, heart-shaped box of chocolates and maybe some flowers too or something else special.

Husbands and wives, love your spouse and treat them special. Splurge on them a little. If you have a good spouse, they are well worth it. You will build memories that will last a life time. In the end, you will find as you bless them, that you are the one that is blessed the most. I know that is most certainly true for me. I still remember that special candlelight dinner and kiss!

Tom with his valentine 25 years later.

FORTY-NINE

An Exciting New Adventure

I have seen in life at times where God opens a new door for a person to go through. Sometimes to walk through that door requires prayer, and a big step of faith, especially when we're not used to doing that specific thing.

It was a big step for us two years ago when I started to write this column. I wrote two stories and tried to get them published in a farm magazine. The editor said, "No, I don't want them, but you are an excellent writer."

A short time after that I had to go into town one day to get some parts for a machine we were fixing here. I took my two "rejected stories" along and stopped at the newspaper office and asked to talk to the editor. I told Barry what I wanted to do and gave him my stories to read. He carefully read through them and then headed for the copying machine. On the way he said, "Tom, I'll publish whatever you write." Since then he has, and I must say over these last two years, he has been wonderful to work with. Thanks, Barry.

Over time, more and more small-town newspapers have picked up my column. One of those newspapers has been the *Cumberland Advocate*. A few weeks ago, I received an e-mail from a reader of that paper that said, "Thank you for writing your column. We use it in our church's prayer and Bible study group." I was very surprised at that and thanked her for the encouraging words. I assumed that would be it. Boy, was I wrong!

About a week later, I received another e-mail from Ann asking me, "Do you ever talk at churches? Would you be interested in coming and sharing your experiences with God?"

My response, "On rare occasions I have spoken. Exactly what do you have in mind?"

Well, the church wanted me to come and preach the Sunday morning service in three weeks, but first they wanted to advertise that I was coming so that readers of my column could come and meet me and hear me speak. I told them that I was not a polished speaker, that I was a farmer, but I would be glad to as long as there were no strings attached concerning what I could speak on. They readily agreed. Why did I do it, you ask? Because, I felt strongly in my spirit that the Lord would have me do it.

I worked on my message, and we prayed as a family for the upcoming service. We also prayed for the Lord to bring in the people who He would have be there that day.

Sunday morning came, and the cows knew something was up! For some reason their owners were feeding and milking them one-and-a-half hours earlier than normal. Chores went well, and we left for church a little ahead of schedule. After driving for nearly an hour, we arrived at Hosanna Church of Cumberland.

Having never been there before in our lives and being their featured guests, we really didn't know what to expect. We walked in, and people started to come up to us and greet us as if we were close family. They all seemed to know us, but we didn't know them at all. Then, more people started arriving at church and greeting us and telling us how much they enjoyed our column. They were all so glad to meet us!

People kept coming, and an older lady came up to me just so joyful and happy. Char informed me that she came all the way up from Illinois to meet me and hear me speak! My jaw almost dropped to the floor at that. She went on to say that she got the Cumberland paper just so she could get my column! I thought to myself, "I hope you're not disappointed after hearing me speak today for all the effort you put into getting here." A number of people said they wished they could move in on our farm!

The time came for me to preach my message, "What God has done in my life and what He can do in yours." I was nervous when I started, but then the Spirit of the Lord came upon me, and I preached like I never preached before in my life. I preached straight from my heart and afterwards a fair number of people came up to me and told me how blessed they were by my message.

After the service was over, the ladies of the church put on a fabulous fellowship dinner. It gave us time to meet many more people and visit with them. One thing we kept hearing over and over again was, "Please don't stop writing your column, we are so blessed by it." I assured them I would keep writing.

After eating a full plate of food plus dessert (farmers can work up a big appetite), I started to visit with two older brothers. Alfred and John were now retired, but years before had farmed together. They were very interesting to visit with. One thing that surprised me was in their early years of farming together, all they ever spoke was German. They informed me that that changed after they both got married! They blamed it on their wives! Then they wanted to know if I spoke German. I assured them that I did not. I did let them know, however, that my grandparents years ago could all speak it fluently. When they left though, they had to say, "Good-bye" in German.

We went to church that day to honor the Lord and bless the people. We came away the most blessed of anybody. It is most certainly true when a person gives from their heart, they will be rewarded by the Lord abundantly.

Going to Hosanna Church and meeting so many people who read our column and speaking to them was something totally new to us. It was an adventure that we will remember the rest of our lives. It was a privilege for us. THANK YOU.

FIFTY

It Just Doesn't Work That Way!

As a young child, I always believed what adults told me. I was always taught to tell the truth and so I assumed that adults always told the truth too. On TV a while back, I heard that 99 percent of Americans admit that they lie. How sad and tragic that is! And what is even worse is when teachers lie, especially to the children that they are supposed to be teaching and setting an example to.

I remember as a young child hearing the biblical account of how God created the world and everything therein in six days. I believed it. As a child, I also went to the public school and was taught evolution from early on – that the world was formed by a big bang and that life evolved over millions or billions of years. As a way-young child, I believed both of them to be true.

As I grew older though, I came to realize that they both couldn't be true. These two teachings were totally opposed to each other. One had to be right, the other a lie. But how is a child to know which one is right?

As I grew older, I gave it a fair bit of thought. Did I, and all this around me, come into existence by chance or did an incredible, powerful God do all of this? For years I didn't know. I wanted to know the truth, but how could I?

Over time I came to know beyond the shadow of a doubt

the answer to my question through two different means. The first one was on the farm. On clear nights I would often gaze up into the heavens in wonder and amazement. To see the multitude of stars spread out all across the heavens in such beauty and perfect order made me come to the conclusion that it was impossible for it to happen by chance. God in his tremendous wisdom and power had to do it.

The second means by which I came to see evolution was a big lie was in public school one day when the teacher was teaching us about evolution. She was a strong believer in it, and she let the whole class know it too.

One day in class she was teaching how terrible it was when a species of animals, whether it was a worm, fish or bird, went extinct. That every resource should be expended to keep anything from going extinct. I sat there thinking about this for a couple of minutes, and then a thought flashed through my brain. I raised my hand and she called upon me. I asked, "Why should we spend large resources to save, say a particular bird species, if as you have been teaching us, all the building blocks of life are all still here, and everything evolved from them? If a bird species goes extinct, give it a week or month or year, and it may very well evolve again."

She did not like my question and said, "It doesn't work that way, it takes more time."

To which I replied, "Well, give it five, ten or twenty years then."

To which the rest of the class responded, "Yes, why not?"

By then her face was beet red and in a very loud and stern voice replied, "It just doesn't work that way!"

I knew if I said another word she would send me to the principal's office. But I, along with the rest of the class, realized that day that evolution doesn't work. It doesn't now, and it never did, and it never will in the future. I fully realized then that Genesis 1:1 was the truth when it said, "In the beginning

God created the heaven and the earth." God created this all. Evolution wasn't a "big bang" but a big lie.

Why do people like to believe the big lie instead of the truth? Because in evolution, you are here by chance, and you are accountable to no one as to how you live your life. But if God created you, which He did, then you will have to give account to Him some day on exactly how you lived your life. If you lived in sin and rebellion, your end will be the lake of fire. But if you acknowledge Him as Creator and live for Him, your home will be heaven. I am glad that I finally came to know the truth. Knowing God, my Creator, and following Him has been the most incredible experience of my life. Not only that though, heaven awaits me and the great opportunity to see my Saviour and Creator face to face!

FIFTY-ONE

A Crown of Thorns

My grandfather, Paul K. Heck, farmed almost his whole life. He was one that enjoyed working with livestock and crops. It was a very challenging and rewarding life for him. But as he got older, he started to slow down some and decided it was time to turn the farm over to his son, Leroy, and his family. So at the age of sixty-nine, Grandpa, and Grandma moved to town.

At that young age though, Grandpa couldn't just sit around and do nothing. Since Grandpa still had farming blood in his veins, he started to plant a good-sized garden every year and harvest it. In addition to the garden, he also started to raise a lot of house plants, mainly flowers. I must say he really had a "green thumb." His plants always flourished.

He had one plant though that was totally unique. Where he got it from I have no idea, but he had it for years. It was a Crown of Thorns plant, also referred to as a "Christ Plant." The one he had was the only one that I've ever seen in my life.

Grandpa kept most of his house plants on the south side of his house where there were a lot of windows to let in the sunshine. This was especially important for the plants in the winter time so they could get enough sunshine. It was an ideal location for them.

The Crown of Thorns plant he kept in the corner, out of the

way, so it wouldn't get too much sunshine. I've been told that
this plant is very difficult to grow. There are many things that
can cause this plant to die, such as too much or too little sunshine and moisture. Also the wrong type of soil and the wrong
humidity will kill it. But Grandpa knew how to take care of his
plant! That plant just thrived!

He had it planted in a pot that was twelve to fifteen inches in
diameter. The plant with the pot included stood about three feet
tall. Once in a while, it would get some pretty, little, pinkish-red
flowers on it. As I said earlier, Grandpa kept the plant in the
corner well out of the way, for the reason being it was such a
dangerous plant to have around. Especially if children were in
the house. He didn't want anybody getting hurt on that plant.

I remember one time when I stopped in to see him, he was
taking care of all his plants. I spotted his Crown of Thorns plant
in the corner and knelt down to examine it. It was the most
wicked bunch of canes with thorns on that I had ever seen in
my life. The thorns were one to two inches long and sharp as
needles! The thorns were so thick you couldn't find any place
on a cane where you could even place one finger. It was totally
impossible! I have to say that on my farm here over the years I
have seen many nasty, thorny plants in my woods, but none of
them compare with Grandpa's plant when it comes to all the
terrible thorns on it!

But Grandpa liked his unique plant. He came over to me and
we started to talk about it. He told me it was a real challenge to
take care of it. Every once in a while, he would prune the canes
back some, and then he would wrap them around each other
going upwards. I think he had some sticks stuck in the pot for
the canes to climb upwards on. There were lots of canes, and he
had them climbing in a circle about eighteen inches in diameter up to about three feet tall. He did a fabulous job with it.

I asked him, "How do you do it with so many wicked thorns?"

He replied, "I use extremely heavy leather fencing gloves and then I have to be real careful! It usually takes me two to three hours when I have to do a full pruning job on it." By looking at the plant, I knew he was telling the truth!

Every year the week before Easter, Grandpa would take his plant to church and put it in the center up front. It always added a lot to services for that week. Virtually everybody would look at that plant and just shudder!

It's almost impossible to comprehend the Roman soldiers taking a bunch of canes off of that plant and weaving them into a circle and pressing them down on Christ's head! Yet Jesus allowed it and went all the way to Calvary where He was crucified on a cross. Why did He do it, you ask? Because He loved us so much that he wanted to redeem us back to our heavenly Father.

After Easter Sunday, Grandpa would take his plant home for another year. The church would always put a big "Thank you" in the bulletin to him for bringing his Crown of Thorns plant to church and sharing it with everybody. I think he earned it!

In Grandpa's latter years when the plant got to be too much for him to take care of, he tried to give it away to anybody in the church that would take it. Nobody would take that plant with all its wicked thorns. I remember it was still in Grandpa's house years later when he died.

Grandpa's Crown of Thorns plant may be gone now, but my Saviour who wore the thorns isn't. Since I repented of my sins and asked Him to come into my life and be my Lord and Saviour, He lives in my heart today. That's what makes life worth living for me.

FIFTY-TWO

Grandpa's Team

Spring is a real special time of year for farmers. It's nice to have the cold snowy winter months behind and to be looking forward to planting seeds in the ground. As the temperature warms up, farmers start to look to the fields wondering how soon they can start to do their spring planting. I believe a farmer's blood gets flowing through his veins faster when it's time to get to the fields with his planting equipment and seed. I know mine does!

I always look at the seeds that I plant as small miracles. It always amazes me how I can take a few bags of seed out to a field and plant them in the spring and then in the fall reap such a bountiful crop. It is truly a miracle of God to have such a multiplication of the seeds that were sown.

I usually work the ground first, getting a nice seed bed, and then I go back and plant it. Over the years, on occasion I have run out of daylight before I have finished planting a particular field. For me though, that generally isn't a problem; I can turn on the lights on my tractor and keep going until I get the field done.

When that happens to me, I always think back to my grandpa. For the first twenty to thirty years of his farming career, he used horses. That was pretty much before the days of tractors. So what did farmers do back then when it got dark on them while they were planting a field, you ask? They would head their team of horses home and hope it won't rain in the night. If it did rain in the night, they would have to go back and rework the part of the field that wasn't planted and then finish planting it. A lot of extra work.

But my grandpa was the exception to the rule. He told me that darkness didn't stop him from finishing a field. My grandfather had a special helper that always helped him after dark so that he could always finish the field he was working on. And no, his helper did not have a flashlight or lantern either. And Grandpa never paid him overtime wages.

Who was this exceptional worker, you ask? His faithful, loving, white farm dog! When the neighboring farmers would head home at dark, Grandpa would stay out in the field with his horses and dog till he finished the field.

Grandpa had his dog trained to run along the edge of what was already planted, and the horses knew to follow just off to the side of the dog. The horses and the dog got along perfectly, and since the dog was white, the horses could see him to follow him even on the darkest nights! Grandpa said he finished planting many a field that way.

The neighbors always shook their heads in disbelief, but what was planted in the dark looked just as good as what was planted in daylight. No skips or gaps or overlapping to speak of. The dog, horses and Grandpa always knew just what to do! In the middle of the night when it stormed, they all slept well, knowing they had the field all planted. They worked in perfect harmony.

Grandpa and his team worked excellent together and accomplished more than could be expected because they worked in harmony, each doing their part. On the farm here, I have often been amazed at how much we can get done in a day when we

GRANDPA'S TEAM

as a family, work in love and harmony with a common goal in mind, each of us doing our very best.

I have seen many families over the years, farm and non-farm alike, that live and work in strife and confusion. How sad this is since it doesn't have to be this way. It is so much better to walk in the love of God and in harmony with one another. It builds the most wonderful relationships imaginable and makes life really worth living. Even Grandpa's horses and dog were living proof of that!

FIFTY-THREE

Buried Treasure

Several years ago, we decided to buy a metal detector to use on our farm. Sometimes after working on a silo unloader, we use it to look for lost nuts or bolts in the feed. It also comes in handy at times for finding metal pieces after working on a piece of machinery in the grass or dirt. It has proven itself very useful and valuable over the years for which we are very thankful.

Besides using it for work though, it has been a lot of fun to play around with treasure hunting. We as a family enjoy doing fun stuff together. Joanne and I have seen over the years that with all the pressure the world puts on young people today, it is vitally important for parents to be good role models to their children and to be good friends to them too. By so doing, children will be greatly blessed, and it will help them go in the right direction in life.

After we bought our metal detector, we started searching for buried treasure all over the farm here. We found lots of junk! Piles of rusty nails and bottle caps to old bent-up silverware to spent bullet cartridges. Once in a while our detector would give off a different signal, that's when we would get excited. Would it be a twenty-dollar gold piece? Or would it be a silver dollar? We never knew until one of us dug down and found the prize.

We never did find a gold or silver piece, but we did find some old brass water valves and small pieces of copper at times.

We did find money once though, we found a quarter dated from the 1970s. It had been in the ground a long time because it had lost all its shine. Since it was only worth twenty-five cents and not in the best condition, we put it back into circulation. Hopefully that helped the US economy out!

One evening in the summer time after we had milked the cows and fed them, we still had good daylight left, so the kids and I decided to go treasure hunting again. We chose a spot where years ago the owners of this farm threw out a lot of their junk.

Then it happened. We were digging down, finding some real treasures, when Joanne came up behind us wanting one of us to come help her with something. The kids excitedly replied, "But, Mom, we're finding buried treasure!" The saying, "one man's junk is another man's treasure," is most certainly true.

What did we find, you ask? We found two old US army medals. I ended up doing a lot of research on them and came to the conclusion that the recipient had served in World War II, Korea or Vietnam.

Apparently, after the war veteran returned home here, he didn't think much of the medals he received and threw them away. The medals were still in pretty good shape, considering how long they had been in the earth. It appears though, that he was somewhat hard on them before he threw them away.

I know many war veterans suffered greatly in serving our country. Many of them returned home very bitter and disillusioned. I think that was the case of the veteran that threw his medals away here.

I, along with many Americans, want to say to all the veterans, both living and dead, "Thank you very much for serving our country so faithfully so that we can enjoy all the freedoms and privileges that we have been so blessed with. Your service was not in vain."

As for the two old war medals we found here, I'm keeping them. Even though I could not find out who the man was that received them, I think highly of him. For it took a lot for him to leave his family and farm behind and go and serve on a foreign field of war. To him and to all who have served in the past and are currently serving, we owe a great debt of gratitude.

FIFTY-FOUR

Tractor Fire!

O n the farm here, we have many jobs that we do together as a family. Being able to work alongside each other and help one another is a privilege that we don't take for granted. It is priceless to us. One of those jobs in the spring of the year is rock-picking.

Rock-picking is hard dirty work, especially if we have a lot of them to pick. Most years it takes three to six days to pick them all. If we don't pick the rocks, they are very hard on the crop harvesting equipment and that can get to be very expensive. So we gladly go out into our fields and pick them.

Sometimes the totally unexpected happens. Sometimes it's a nice surprise and other times it isn't. A while back, we had one of those surprises that wasn't so nice.

When we go rock-picking, we put one of our older, smaller tractors on the trailer that we use to throw the rocks into. This spring we had our old dependable Farmall Super M on it. On this particular day, I got the Super M out of the shed with the trailer hooked behind it. I drove it up by the house to pick up Joanne and the kids.

Joanne, being the wonderful wife and mother that she is, would always pack a light lunch with some treats and some- thing to drink. A lot of times she would take a two-liter bottle of pop along to drink. On this day though, she did it different. She poured the pop into a thermos jug instead. I was surprised she did it, but she thought it would be nicer to drink out of.

We got loaded up and headed down the road to the field. Since it was a half mile to our field road, I put the tractor in "road gear" and gave it full throttle – wide open. It didn't take long to get down to our field road at that speed. But just before I got to the field road, flames started to shoot out from under the hood! I had never had an experience like this before in my life. I got the tractor off of the blacktop road and onto the field road as fast as I could and hit the brakes. I jumped off the tractor and asked Joanne for the thermos. It wasn't much to fight a fire with, but it was all that I had. I ran up alongside the tractor engine where the flames were bellowing out by now. It was a dangerous situation since the flames were getting close to the gas tank. I took the top off of the thermos and thrust the pop up under the hood with great force, aiming it at the exhaust manifold which seemed to be the hottest part of the fire.

I was amazed at the results. It nearly quenched the whole fire! I set the thermos down and unhooked the hood as fast as I could and lifted it up. I knew I didn't have any time to waste since I didn't have any more pop to use if it flared up again. Once I got the hood up, I saw the reason for the fire.

Some very industrious birds had taken a bunch of sticks and dry hay and built a big nest on top of the exhaust manifold. When the manifold got hot, it started the large nest on fire. I reached up in there with gloves on and cleaned out the rest of the nest and got the fire put out completely.

Breathing a lot easier now, I put the hood back down and picked up the thermos. My good jug was busted. Apparently, I hit it hard on the tractor when I threw the pop up in. Our thermos was junk, and our pop for the day was gone, but we were all so thankful that the fire was out. We had saved our old dependable Super M, and none of us had gotten hurt. The only damage to it was that the hood was darkened from the fire.

What were Joanne and the kids doing while I fought the fire? Praying. It pays to pray! We pray over ourselves, our farm and equipment every day. We know our heavenly Father hears our prayers and answers them. If He didn't, we wouldn't pray. I think it's a miracle that Joanne put the pop in the thermos that day because she never did that before! If it would have been in the bottle, I could never have gotten it up onto the fire. Furthermore, to put out that large of a fire with just two liters of pop is almost unbelievable. But our God does the unbelievable when we pray! I like what the Bible says in Ephesians 3:20, "He is able to do exceeding abundantly above all that we ask or think." I'm so glad to know a loving God that does!

FIFTY-FIVE

She's a Dead Cow – Don't Call Me Anymore!

We have a small herd of dairy cows on our farm here. Each one has her own name and she knows it. Whenever a heifer calf is born here, we give her a name that she will have the rest of her life. We always like to give the calf a name that starts with the same letter as her mother's name does. That way it is easier to keep track of each one's lineage. Sometimes, it's a challenge coming up with new names for new calves. Sometimes we come up with some real unique names. Years ago once, when we had a beautiful heifer calf born here, we came up with the name "Kangkle."

Sometimes a farmer gets a cow that he remembers all the rest of his life. Kangkle was such a cow. She grew up and became one of my better producing cows. She was a big, beautiful Holstein cow that had a friendly personality all her own. She got to be special to all of us early in her life.

Then one year in March, she gave birth to a real nice calf and started milking really good. But, shortly after this, one day I noticed she wouldn't hardly eat anything. It was obvious she was sick. I took her temperature and it was sky high! Lots of times I can diagnose what is wrong with a cow and treat her myself. But this time I was baffled. We then as a family prayed asking God for healing for her.

I called the vet up and he came out and examined her. He was just as puzzled as I was. One thing was for sure, we had to get her fever down. We gave her an IV of powerful antibiotics, and the vet thought that would take care of it.

Unfortunately, the vet was wrong. The next day Kangkle still had a high temperature and would only nibble at her feed. We treated her again and kept praying. The sad thing is that the days turned into weeks with no improvement. We all felt sorry for her, and yet we were doing all we could possibly do. Kangkle got to the place where she looked just terrible. She looked like a bag of bones.

If this wasn't bad enough, I had another young cow calve in that got sick just like Kangkle, just not quite as severe. Finally, after running up a large vet bill, the vet said to me one day after treating Kangkle, "She's a dead cow – don't call me anymore. As far as that other one goes, I don't think she will live either."

I replied, "How will Kangkle die?"

He answered, "You will come in here sometime soon and find her dead, or she will be so weak that she wouldn't be able to get up anymore and then will have to be put to sleep."

The situation looked absolutely hopeless, but I know with God there is always hope. We as a family kept praying for our sick cows, and I took over treating them completely. I knew I couldn't call the vet anymore, so I used my best judgment in treating them. Kangkle held onto life by a thread, and then her fever started to slowly drop, and she started to eat more along with my other cow. In time I was able to quit the antibiotics on both of them and their temperatures returned to normal. We were all so thankful to the Lord for saving both of our cows.

Kangkle was alive, but she was very weak and looked terrible. She got her full appetite back and really went to eating along with the other one. We fed them the best feed that we had, and they started to put weight back on and produce milk again.

Then it happened one day when I was feeding Kangkle, I

heard an inner voice say to me, "She is my cow." I thought it was strange and just brushed it off. But a couple days later when I was feeding her again, I heard the same words. This time I knew it was the Lord speaking.

I replied out loud, "Lord, if she is your cow what do I do with her?"

The answer came back immediately, "You can milk her as long as she is profitable and then when you sell her, I get the money."

I responded, "O.K., Lord."

I realized that if He hadn't answered our prayers, both of those cows would have been dead. So if He wanted one of them, He was certainly entitled to one. But He chose the worst looking cow in the whole barn! Kangkle! She was just a bunch of skin and bones. I thought He could have chosen a lot better one, but I didn't argue with Him. I learned a long time ago not to question God. A lot of people would be much better off if they didn't question God.

Well, Kangkle went to eating and eating, I guess she knew she had to make up for all she had lost. Everybody here knew she wasn't our cow anymore. We all referred to her as "The Lord's Cow." So we all treated her extra special.

In time Kangkle put all the weight back on that she had lost. She got to be the best looking cow that we had in the barn! Over time a number of people walked down the aisle in my barn – electricians, plumbers, carpenters, feed men, neighbors and friends. And it happened over and over again. They would stop talking about whatever they were talking about and look at Kangkle and say, "What a beautiful cow." I never in all my life had a cow get so many compliments from others as she did after the Lord restored her. God can take the worst, most hopeless cases and turn them into something beautiful for His glory.

A number of months later, when Kangkle was in her prime, I had to have the vet out for something minor on a different cow. As the vet was outside the barn getting ready to leave, he turned to me and said, "Whatever happened to that cow I treated this last spring?"

I replied, "She's in the barn there right now."

He looked straight at me and said, "She can't be."

I responded, "Come on back into the barn and I'll show her to you."

With that he kept shaking his head and saying, "She can't be. She can't be." I urged him to come back into the barn and look at her, but he refused and kept shaking his head saying, "She can't be. She can't be." With that he got into his truck and left.

We milked Kangkle for a long time after that, but the time came when she was no longer profitable to milk. So the day came when we sold her. It was hard to do, but we knew it was the right thing to do. The Lord guided us where to give the money, which we did. He used it to help two people out and radically change their lives, for which we give God the glory.

The vet said, "She's a dead cow, don't call me anymore." In the natural he was right; Kangkle was a cow beyond hope. But we serve a God where nothing is impossible. The Word of God is most certainly true in Luke 18:27 where it says, "The things which are impossible with men are possible with God." Kangkle was next to dead, yet God raised her up and made her the most beautiful cow in the whole barn. I have never received so many compliments on a cow in all my years of farming as I received on her.

God is still in the restoration business today. He takes people in utterly hopeless situations that cry out to Him and makes something beautiful out of their lives for His glory. If He did it for Kangkle, how much more wouldn't He do it for a person? I tell you He will do it much more so. I'm living proof of it!

FIFTY-SIX

Having Fun with the Kids

We have an old Gehl chopper box that we use for filling our silos with haylage and corn silage. We also use it for putting up lots of cornstalk bedding in the fall for our dairy cattle. We bought it used about twenty years ago. At that time it was at least ten years old already. Since we were heavily in debt then, we couldn't dream of buying new! But that didn't bother us, we were so thankful to find a nice used one in excellent condition. We knew that we had to live within our means, so we got it. We've never regretted it. If more Americans today would live within their means, it would save them a lot of heartache and grief.

It has been a very reliable piece of equipment these many years. Apart from a few breakdowns, it has served us well. We have sought to take excellent care of it so that it would last. Most chopper boxes the age of ours have been junked-out long ago.

But, after over thirty years of dependable service, things do wear out. The cross conveyor chain that unloads the feed and bedding into the blower or elevator was worn out. Since the rest of the box looked really good yet, we decided to fix it instead of getting a different box. We knew by doing this it would save us a lot of money. So I, along with my kids, Catherine and Joshua, decided to fix it.

Well, the job turned out to be a lot more expensive and difficult than we had expected. New parts have gone up drastically in price in the last few years. As we got tearing it apart, we came to see that we needed more parts than what we had originally figured. Plus, other parts had to get welded up and rebuilt at a local blacksmith shop. By the time we had paid for the new parts and the blacksmith's bill, we had spent over a thousand dollars. Far more than what I had planned.

As I said earlier, it was more difficult to do than what we had expected. When sprockets have been on shafts for over thirty years, they don't want to move! That's where a neighbor with a cutting torch and forty-ton press comes in real handy!

Well, we got it all apart. We then got the new parts from the implement shop along with the rebuilt parts. The day came to put it all back together. A lot easier said than done! But, we did get it done and working excellently. Along the way, we ended up replacing all the roller chains that drive the box too. I originally figured it would take a couple days to fix, but it ended up taking over a week and being much more challenging.

Was it worth doing, you ask? Absolutely. Hopefully it will run another thirty years. There was a big dividend with it too. What was that, you ask? The fun I had working on it with my kids!

I was impressed, every day the kids wanted to get the chores done as fast as they could so that we could get to work on the box. They also didn't want to spend any extra time eating dinner. They greatly enjoy fixing stuff with Dad! Especially when they can see it's necessary and profitable. They think its great fun. They would rather do that than play a game. I must admit too, that I enjoy fixing things with them.

I have let them help me ever since they were old enough to hand me wrenches. I have always sought to treat them with love and respect and teach them all that I know. Because of that, I have two wonderful helpers now. The Bible is certainly correct when it says in Proverbs 22:6, "Train up a child in the way he should go: and when he is old, he will not depart from it."

I must say it is truly wonderful working with my family here and enjoying it every day. As we have followed the Scriptures over the years, we all have been greatly blessed. If you will do it in your family, you also will reap the rewards of a life blessed by God. I know that I have. Every time we use the old chopper box, I look back fondly at the time I spent with my kids, fixing it up.

FIFTY-SEVEN

Special Guests

Just two days ago, we had the honor of having a family from Mexico visit us on our farm. Alberto and Ann Aguilar, along with their three sons, Lucas, Evan and Matthew made the drive from Minnesota. It was the first time for them to be on a dairy farm in Wisconsin.

The kids and I were working in the shop when they drove into the yard. While we were still greeting them, ten-year-old Matthew headed off to the sheds to see the machinery. We decided we had better all follow him. Once in the sheds, Alberto started asking me all kinds of questions about different pieces of machinery. I did my best to answer all his questions.

He started looking at my two oldest tractors and thought they looked fairly new. He was shocked when I told him they were both over fifty years old! I explained that we try to buy good equipment, and then we seek to take excellent care of it so that it lasts for many years.

We went to the barn and showed them our cattle. Alberto was very interested in them since he is a licensed veterinarian in Mexico. He had many questions since farming here is so different than where he comes from. Finally after finishing our tour of the farm here, we sat down for dinner. We have a large picnic table that we put under our giant white oak tree so that we could eat in the shade and visit together.

Joanne made a large hot dish to serve along with sweet corn and tomatoes from our garden. While we were eating and visiting, one of our cats named Mr. Stripey jumped up on the bench between Catherine and Alberto and put his front paws up on the table. He started to eat Alberto's ear of sweet corn! We were shocked. Alberto in a very nice way picked up Mr. Stripey and the ear of sweet corn and put them both on the ground. With that our cat was very satisfied. Needless to say, that wasn't supposed to happen.

We got talking about them and the work that they do. They are from a mining town up in the mountains of central Mexico where there is little agriculture. It is a very dry, barren area. There are a few chickens around, along with an occasional pig or cow. They do grow a few vegetables and fruit trees, but that is about it. The area is basically a semi-desert with lots of cactus. We noticed that the boys were amazed at how green our farm is here.

In their town up in the mountains, there is a mine that runs seven days a week around the clock. They mine mainly copper along with small amounts of lead, silver and gold. They do use modern machinery in the mining process today. They also use dynamite on a daily basis. It is never quiet where they live unless the mine shuts down for some unexpected reason.

Now, for the most interesting part of this story. Ann was raised in Minnesota. As a small girl, she gave her life to the Lord and sought to follow Him. She attended a university in Minnesota and worked with Teen Challenge for a while. Later, in 1994, God called her to Mexico to the mining town that she now calls home.

She started preaching the gospel in this town of 4,000 people where there was no gospel witness. Some young Christian men started to come and help her at times. One of them, Alberto, on one occasion brought her twenty beautiful red roses. They were married in 1995.

Alberto is also a pastor, and together they minister to the people in the town. The town's people are very poor and live in great spiritual darkness. Drugs, prostitution, alcoholism, witchcraft and idolatry are many of the powerful forces that enslave the people. But by living among the people and teaching them the Word of God, lives are being transformed.

I asked Ann, "Why do you do it?"

Her answer: "God would have me do it. I wanted to be where no one was doing the work of God. Everyone needs to know how much Jesus loves them."

Our Lord said in Mark 16:15, "Go ye into all the world, and preach the gospel to every creature." Alberto and Ann have followed the command of our Lord and are preaching the gospel in a remote part of the world. They are an inspiration to us here. We are privileged to know them and to have had them to our farm. As evening set in, we bid our friends farewell and went to feed and milk our cows. They said that they were so blessed to come and share the day with us, but we were the most blessed of all.

A special day on our farm with the Aguilars. Front row left to right: Catherine, Joanne, Matthew and Evan. Back row: Joshua, Tom, Alberto and Ann. Photo by Lucas.

FIFTY-EIGHT

Only One Chance in Ten?

We went through a very busy season here lately, calving in a lot of cows and heifers. We always seek to watch them closely and assist them when they need it. Often times, my wonderful wife Joanne will get up in the middle of the night to check on our due ones. I'm so blessed to have such a caring, hardworking wife to work alongside of.

The calvings all went well, except for one. Our cow, Flower, went into labor on her due date, but early on it became evident that things were not well. The calf was coming backwards, and it was an extra-large one at that. The four of us assisted Flower in having her calf. We prayed as we worked, and the Lord answered our prayers, we delivered a very large male calf. In situations like this, often times the calf is born dead. This one was very much alive though, for which we thanked the Lord.

Shortly thereafter, Flower stood up, so we gave our "Little Giant" his first meal. He was one hungry baby! This all happened around noon on Friday. Later that evening when we came to milk Flower she was lying down. She tried to get up but could only raise herself up a few inches.

I figured she had "milk fever" which is a condition cows get sometimes after they calve. After calving, cows start to produce milk which is high in calcium. Sometimes they drain their bodies way low on calcium. When they do this, their muscles will not function properly, and they cannot stand up. The solution to this is to IV a bottle of liquid calcium into their neck vein. The kids and I proceeded to do this while Joanne milked the other cows.

It is normal within thirty minutes of giving a cow calcium in this manner for them to stand up. Flower tried, but could do no better than before. We all knew then that we had a major problem. I then called up our vet on the phone and told him what the situation was. He told me that I had done the right thing in giving Flower the calcium, but obviously she had a much more serious problem. I already knew that. The vet went on and said, "By having such a large calf she probably bruised her muscles terribly bad and may have pinched some nerves also. The best thing you can do for her is to get her out of the barn and onto pasture. The chances of her making it though are very slim. I wish I had better news for you, but that's it." I thanked him and said good-bye.

Immediately we went to work getting Flower out of the barn. We have a cow sled that we built in the past out of heavy plywood and oak planks for situations like this. With Catherine holding the flashlight, Joshua and I got the sled out of the corner of the pole shed and up to the barn. Then we got our old dependable Farmall tractor with a log chain up to the barn also.

Then we were ready for the hardest part of the job, getting our 1,500-pound Flower out of the stall and onto the sled. She had had a very hard day already and did not want to cooperate. But with lots of prayer, patience and hard work, we got her onto the sled. I then jumped onto the tractor and pulled my heavy sled a hundred yards out to pasture. Once there, we got her off and left.

It was nearly midnight when we finally got into the house. Sometimes farming requires long days and nights, but we don't mind; we gladly do the work the Lord has given us to do. We count it a privilege to farm and serve Him in it. Before we went to bed that night, we prayed as a family asking the Lord to restore Flower to full health. Jesus said in John 16:24, "Ask and ye shall receive, that your joy may be full." We asked in faith, and we knew our joy would be very full when Flower would once again be on her own feet roaming the pastures. We knew in the natural though, it really looked hopeless. But we serve a God that does the impossible.

The next day Joshua started taking feed and water out to Flower. He kept doing this every day even though we saw very little if any improvement in her condition. And yes, we kept praying as a family every day for the Lord to fully restore her. Finally, one week later on Friday, Flower stood on her feet once again! We were all so elated and just thanked the Lord for answering our prayers and raising Flower up.

Today, Flower is back to her old normal self, roaming the pastures and coming up to the barn. The other day I crossed paths with our vet. I told him that our cow had made it. He was surprised and said, "Only about one out of ten down cows like that make it."

To which I replied, "We prayed and believed God to restore her so her chances were far higher." He didn't have much of a comment to make to that.

I must say that it is wonderful serving God. He commands us to pray and then lovingly answers our prayers showing Himself strong on our behalf. Flower is living proof of that!

Flower in the pasture today.

FIFTY-NINE

An Old Veteran

Recently, Catherine and I attended a farm business meeting in Jim Falls. As we drove into that town we saw a large statue of a famous Civil War Veteran. This brave veteran took part in forty-two battles and skirmishes with bullets flying all around him. This leader was so popular that they changed the name of the regiment from Badger to Eagle after him. Who was he, you ask? Old Abe, the war eagle. There has never been another bald eagle like him before or since.

Old Abe was born in the early spring of 1861 about twenty-five miles north of Jim Falls. The Chippewa Indians that resided north of there a ways would always collect maple sap and boil it down to maple sugar to take down river in their birch bark canoes to trade for supplies. On the way down river, Chief Sky's group saw an eagle hovering around a tall pine tree.

So one of the young braves climbed up the tree to get the young eaglets in hopes of trading them for supplies also. As the man got close to the nest, the mother eagle attacked him to protect her young ones. The Indians shot her dead, and the brave proceeded to get the two young eagles out of the nest. God, the Creator, put it into the heart of the mother eagle to protect her young at all costs, even to the point of death. It is sad to see that so many parents don't protect their children from the evil and dangers in the world today. Because of it, the children pay a terrible price.

The Indians proceeded down river and stopped at a small farm owned by Dan McCann and his wife. The McCanns had just finished planting their corn and had about a half bushel of seed left over. The Indians offered to trade one of the young eagles for the leftover seed, but when Mrs. McCann saw the bird, she was convinced it was a crow and wanted nothing to do with it! Young eagles are solid black and do not get their white feathers until they are two to three years old. The Indians insisted that it was a bald eagle and went down to one of their canoes and brought up the dead mother. When she saw it, she changed her mind and made the trade.

Dan McCann played the fiddle very well, and the eagle loved it. He would walk around and dance and flutter his wings to the music. The eagle grew and by late summer had become a large bird. A company of soldiers was being formed in the area to go and fight. Dan wanted to go but couldn't since he was a cripple, so he sent the eagle in his place. The company gladly accepted him as their mascot and changed their name from the Badger Company to the Eagle Company. They also named their new member "Old Abe" in honor of President Abraham Lincoln.

Old Abe rode on a special perch next to the flags. This usually put him in the worst part of the battle. Most birds, at the sound of a gun, would seek to fly away to safety, but not Old Abe. He lived for battle! History tells us that the hotter the battle got, the more he would flutter his large wings and let out shrill screams that could be heard above the sound of battle. His courage gave the men great inspiration to fight even harder, sometimes against overwhelming odds.

Confederate Generals Price and Van Dorn commanded their armies to take Old Abe dead or alive. They knew if they could get him, it would have a very demoralizing effect on the union armies. Old Abe was kept up front by the flags at all times and had tons of bullets flying around him, yet he only lost some of his wing feathers. I think the Lord must have preserved his life, especially when you consider that in the battle of Corinth, the regiment lost fifty percent of its men.

When General Grant and other Union Generals would pass by Old Abe, they would salute him like he was President Lincoln and raise their hats to him. At this the Wisconsin regiment would let out loud cheers, and Old Abe would spread his magnificent wings. The generals along with all the other men loved it; it motivated them to keep going on, even on bad days.

After the war, Old Abe returned to Wisconsin and made many public appearances to raise money for veterans. He was always the honored guest at such meetings. On his last appearance in Milwaukee in 1880, he met his old friend General Grant. The two old warriors had a great love and respect for each other. In March of 1881, the famous war eagle died. It is said that many veterans cried when they heard about his death.

If Old Abe would have been left in his nest when he was young, he would have had a normal life like other eagles. But circumstances beyond his control totally changed his life. So it is in life for many people: circumstances beyond our control change our lives radically. I know that has certainly been true in my life. I am so glad though to know the Lord. The Bible says in Romans 8:28, "We know that all things work together for good to them that love God, to them who are the called according to his purpose." Since I belong to Him and follow Him, He makes all things to work out for my good. He will do it for you too, if you will give Him your life. I must say it is the most exciting and rewarding life possible. I'm sure Old Abe would agree with that.

Catherine standing in front of Old Abe's statue.

SIXTY

The Most Wonderful Time of the Year

The most wonderful time of the year for us is Christmas time. The crops to feed our cattle are all put up for another year. Even though we had a drought this year, the Lord still blessed us with enough to see us through another winter. For which we are extremely thankful. We know of farmers and ranchers in other parts of the country that suffered much more than what we did, and our hearts and prayers go out to them.

We are also blessed to have our firewood all put up for another year. We have one very large pile of it this year. We heat our house and all the hot water we use in it and in our milk house with an outdoor, wood-burning furnace. So, needless to say, it takes a lot of wood. But, it also saves a lot of money. What's more, we as a family enjoy working together doing it.

So here we are now in December, we just cut a Christmas tree out of our woods a few days ago and have it decorated in our living room. As I write this, it is lit up with all different colors of lights. It also has all kinds of different ornaments on it along with plenty of tinsel. Joanne and Catherine did a beautiful job of decorating it this year again. So far it only has two presents under it, but I know there will be many more coming.

It is always a blessing buying good gifts for the ones we love. Our tree also gets extra presents under it since Joshua's and my birthdays are both in December. Our birthday presents always end up under one side of the tree separate from the Christmas presents.

It always seems like there is extra love, joy and peace in our home at this time of year as we prepare to celebrate Christmas. It's a privilege to go out every day and take care of the cows and all the young stock. Catherine has once again set up a small Christmas tree outside the barn for all the cats. The cats seem to enjoy it every year!

And then it comes – Christmas Day. We once again go out and milk the cows and feed all the cattle. We always try to treat them extra special on this day, and they know it. The cows will moo softly and nuzzle us with their noses. We put our arms around their heads and pet them softly. We treat them special because they are special to us. And of course, we treat each other extra special too.

Once we have our chores done, we go in and have a wonderful Christmas dinner that Joanne has so lovingly prepared. After this, we sit down and read the biblical account of how God gave the greatest gift ever given to us – Jesus. He is the whole reason for Christmas. Without Him, there would be no Christmas. No giving gifts to each other. No Christmas tree. There would be no peace with God. There would be no answers to our prayers. There would be no relationship with Him and certainly no thoughts of making heaven our home.

But because Jesus was born in a stable for us, we have the greatest gift in the whole universe. Because He came, we celebrate Christmas. We have life and that so much more abundantly.

It has been a privilege sharing our lives with you this past year again. We hope this has been a blessing to you. From our home to yours, we wish you the most blessed Christmas.

Tom petting Bossie.

SIXTY-ONE

Why Did This Happen?

This morning as I sat in the kitchen putting my work shoes on, I turned on the TV news. The news anchor woman was interviewing another woman who was supposed to be an expert on how to handle tragedies. They were talking about the terrible tragedy that had happened at Sandy Hook Elementary School in Newtown, Connecticut. Twenty young children along with six adults were killed by a lone gunman.

The anchor woman shared how her young daughter asked her, "Why did this happen?"

To which the mother replied, "I don't know."

The anchor woman then turned to the expert and asked her the same question, "Why did this happen?"

The expert's reply was the same, "I don't know." The expert went on to say that we need to talk to our children and ask them, "Why do you think this happened?" She thought it would be good to get the children to talk about it.

The next thing that came up was that a lot of children all across America are not going to feel safe going back to school. The expert's response was that we need to tell the children that it will be safe for them to go back to school because we have lots of policemen, teachers, principals and others to protect them. By this time, I had put my shoes on, so I shut the TV off, shaking my head in disbelief as I headed out to take care of my cattle.

When we as a family, heard of this great tragedy the previous afternoon, I immediately turned to my family and said, "I can tell you exactly why this happened." Then I went on to say, "This nation has put God out of the schools and out of public life as much as possible. They want nothing to do with God and His ways anymore. When you put God and His ways out, then the devil and his cohorts work totally unobstructed in their ways. Their ways are lying, stealing, cheating, drugs, immorality, death and destruction. This nation put God out of the public schools many years ago. When He got put out, the devil had free rein to do his work. Now, after many years, it's come to all this death and destruction."

The Bible sums this up very well in John 10:10 when Jesus said, "The thief cometh not, but for to steal, and to kill, and to destroy: I am come that they might have life, and that they might have it more abundantly."

The expert's second answer about telling the children they will be safe going back to school because of all the policemen, teachers, principals and others out there to protect them is so hollow and empty. Those people were all present in Newtown, Connecticut, but it didn't save the lives of the twenty children that perished that day. Likewise, many other children have died in school shootings over the years. So why do we think they will be able to save the children in the future?

Why can't a teacher in public school today put on the blackboard the commandment from God, "Thou shall not kill" or "Love thy neighbor as thyself"? It would help children to grow up right. To respect life and to help others, not kill them! But in America today, a court would rule that the teacher couldn't do that because it would be violating somebody's constitutional

WHY DID THIS HAPPEN?

rights! If the teacher didn't remove God's Word, he/she would be fired and maybe end up in jail!

So today, God is out of the public schools, and the devil is firmly entrenched there. Is it any wonder that we see so much immorality, drugs, violence, suicide and death among our students today? The Bible says in Hosea 8:7, "For they have sown the wind, and they shall reap the whirlwind."

Will things get better in America now that this has happened? Absolutely not. It will only get worse. We as a nation will continue to reap the harvest of putting God out of our public schools and public life. It is very, very sad to realize this, but I say it with tears that it is most certainly true.

What should we do, seeing we live in such dangerous times? We need to be reading our Bibles and teaching our families the Word of God. We also need to obey the Word of God. This will teach our children to do the same. Last, but not least, we need to pray for God's protection over us and our children every day. God can and will watch over our children when we ask Him to, even when policemen, teachers and others cannot. I realize we live in dangerous times, but I know God is more than able to take care of us and our children. We must look to Him and trust Him every day.

SIXTY-TWO

A Bold, Cold Step of Faith

Sometimes in life we are called to take a big bold step of faith. Such was the case for Joanne and myself in early 1991. I was working as a hired man on my parents' dairy farm then, but they had informed us months before already that they wanted us out. I didn't know it at the time, but they were turning the farm over to my older brother Paul.

So for a number of months, we had earnestly sought the Lord daily as to what He had for us. Through much prayer, He made known to us that He had a farm for us. We didn't know where it was, but we did know He had one for us. We knew if we were going to farm, we needed a line of farm machinery. I owned absolutely none!

We prayed and felt led that I should start to attend farm auctions in the area to buy old used farm machinery to farm the farm the Lord had promised us. We started to look at the farm newspapers for auction bills. The first auction we came across was on January 29, 1991, at Kellogg, Minnesota. It had a Farmall 806 diesel tractor on it. I figured it would be a big enough tractor for us to start farming with.

Joanne and I looked at our checkbook; we had just over $5,000 in it. That was all the money we had, except for a few dollars in our wallets. We did not have $5,100 total. Joanne looked at me and asked, "Would that tractor be a good deal for $5,000?"

"If the tractor is in good condition, it would be an excellent deal," I replied. So we got down on our knees and prayed to our heavenly Father asking Him in faith that we could buy that 806 for $5,000. The Bible says in Matt. 18:19, "That if two of you shall agree on earth as touching any thing that they shall ask, it shall be done for them of my Father which is in heaven."

January 29th came, and it was bitter cold. Twenty degrees below zero with a twenty-mile-an-hour wind out of the north. My brother Paul and I went to the auction that day. I was walking in pure faith that day. I knew that if I had missed it with God, I would be going home empty-handed. We got to the farm and headed for the line of tractors. We walked down the line till we got to the 806. Boy, were we disappointed. It was in real rough shape as were the other tractors we had walked by before it. I knew I didn't want that tractor.

But then Paul saw a tractor just beyond it and said, "Hey, look at that one." We looked at it and were greatly impressed. It was a Farmall 1206 diesel in excellent condition! We were shocked because all the rest of the tractors were in such poor condition, and this one stood out like a diamond! What's more, this one was not listed on the auction bill.

The auctioneer kept the auction moving at a real fast pace that day because of the bitter cold. He knew if he didn't he would lose a lot of the bidders. They started all the tractors up; the 1206 ran as nice as it looked. I decided to bid on it. The auctioneer started down the row of tractors; he had a few interested bidders in the 806 and sold it for almost $6,000. I was surprised that it went for that much. Then he came to the 1206 and said the reason it wasn't listed on the bill was because it was sitting in the corner of the shed, and he had missed it.

I didn't believe him, and I think nobody else did either. But, with that he opened up the bidding.

I started bidding right away and the price climbed fast. Soon I had the bid at exactly $5,000 and the auctioneer kept asking for $5,050. I held my breath. I knew if somebody bid that, then the next price would be $5,100 which I did not have. I clearly remembered how Joanne and I had asked the Lord for an 806 tractor for $5,000, and now I was looking at a larger, much better tractor for that miraculous price. I knew if we got it for that price, it most certainly was the Lord answering our prayer. Finally, after what seemed like an eternity, the auctioneer said, "Sold." I had just bought my first tractor.

People in the crowd were shaking their heads in disbelief, trying to comprehend what had just happened. Later on, when I talked to the farmer about the tractor, he also was dumbfounded over the 1206 selling for less than his 806. He just couldn't believe the price the 1206 sold for. He went on to tell me, "That 1206 was my favorite tractor. I let the hired help run all the other tractors here, but I wouldn't let them touch that tractor. I'm the only one that ran that tractor. I had planned on keeping it, but at the last minute decided to sell it also. That's why it wasn't listed on the auction bill."

Paul offered to start driving the tractor home while I went and wrote out a check paying for it. I caught up to him when he was driving it over the bridge crossing the Mississippi River at Wabasha. As soon as he got into Wisconsin, he stopped and came back to the pickup. After driving it just several miles, he looked like he was almost froze up. The tractor did not have a cab on it, so we had nothing protecting us from the cold and wind. Paul asked me, "Do you want to take it up over the bluffs on the back roads and save several miles?"

I said, "Sure, if you will pick out the route with the pickup."

Fortunately, I had dressed well. I was wearing my insulated

coveralls and the sheepskin coat that my grandfather had given me several years earlier. It was the one he had worn decades before when he would go into town with his team of horses in the winter time. Now I was wearing it as I headed my new "red horse" north across the bluffs. Looking back, that was the coldest ride of my life! But it was a wonderful ride. There is such excitement when one steps out in faith and sees God answer above and beyond what one asks for. And that is what God did that day for us.

When we drove it into the yard, Joanne was looking out the window and was surprised at how big and beautiful the tractor looked. When I told her the whole story, she just started praising the Lord with me. God was faithful; He had answered our prayer and more. The Bible is most certainly true when it says in Ephesians 3:20, "[He] is able to do exceeding abundantly above all that we ask or think." It is wonderful to know that when we walk rightly with God, we can pray and fully expect Him to answer our prayers. We are not alone in this world, we have a wonderful, loving heavenly Father to guide us and to provide for us what we have need of.

Tom by his 1206 tractor.

SIXTY-THREE

Don't Forget Your Valentine

That special day is coming up soon again. That special day to tell your sweetheart that you love them and that they are very special. That day of course is Valentine's Day.

In our fast paced world today, it is easy for married couples to start to take each other for granted. The person we should love, honor and respect the most, we often times forget to treat special at all. We should never take for granted the spouse we married and pledged ourselves to.

When a married couple starts to take each other too much for granted, that's when their marriage starts to go downhill. I have a sad, but true story to recount here.

Many years ago, when we were first starting to farm here, I had a good friend who would come sometimes and help me fix machinery. We would naturally visit as we worked on the machinery together. Sometimes we would talk about "Treasure Island" and some of the really good things we got from there.

You ask, "What is Treasure Island?" It's the name we'd given the spot where the city had their place for people to drop off their garbage. Back then, if you could find something of value there, you could freely take it. So we scavengers got all kinds of treasures from there. The phrase "One person's trash is another person's treasure" was true here.

One time my friend, Mike, found a very expensive window in excellent condition there. It appears that it came from a doctor's or lawyer's office when they did a bunch of remodeling. I had a glass block window in my milk house that was literally falling to pieces. When he asked me if I could use his new found treasure, my answer was, "Absolutely yes!"

It took all of my carpentry skills, but I got it fit in there beautifully. This now, is twenty years later, and the window looks as nice now as the day I put it in. It was and still is a super quality window that was sure worth retrieving.

Another time Mike told me of something he'd found at Treasure Island that nearly brought us to tears. He found a large wedding album filled with pictures. The couple in the album had had a large wedding party with many guests. They had a fabulous wedding day with everything done to perfection.

But, what had started out so beautifully and wonderfully had now ended in disaster. The lovely bride and handsome bridegroom in time ended up getting divorced! Their marriage didn't last very long. When they split up, they took a lot of their things, including their wedding album, to the garbage place. How tragic! Mike, when he got done looking at it, gently laid it back in the trash.

Wedding albums should never be put in the garbage. Marriages should never end in divorce either. Broken marriages and broken people and innocent children caught in the fray. It should not be this way. There are way too many broken homes and marriages in our nation today.

We need to keep our wedding vows and love our spouses with all our hearts. We need to love them and treat them special every day, not just on our wedding day. But there are days when we can really treat them special and show them how much we really do love them. One of those days is Valentine's Day. If we do this, there will be a lot fewer wedding albums ending up in the garbage. If we do this, we will be amazed as we look back in time at how blessed we've been.

The Bible says in Luke 6:38, "Give and it shall be given unto you; good measure, pressed down and shaken together and running over." I know that as I have learned to express my love and appreciation to my wife on a daily basis, it has certainly improved our marriage and family life. And in the end, I'm the one blessed most of all. So men, on this Valentine's Day, do something special for your wife that says you really love her and would count it a privilege to marry her all over again!

SIXTY-FOUR

A Matter of Integrity

A while back, our son Joshua got the fever. At first it wasn't too bad, but as time went on, it went from bad to worse. There were times when we tried to cure it that he improved, but in time it would always come back worse than what it had been before. As a father, I did everything I could to help my son get through it without getting burned badly. That can be a real challenge at times though. It took a lot of time and patience to get him through it and successfully cured.

What is this fever, you ask? It's a thing young farm boys get, and the only way to cure it is by them buying a tractor! It's also known as "Tractor Fever." And it isn't always boys that get it either. Sometimes grown men can get extremely bad cases of it! It has to be treated very carefully. Many people have made very bad deals on tractors that later on they've regretted.

Joshua wanted to buy an old Farmall tractor to use on the farm here. I was really glad that he liked the same kind of tractors that I do. I laid down a couple of rules concerning purchasing a used tractor. One was that it had to be in good working condition. That can be a challenge when the tractor we're looking for will be forty to sixty years old! A second condition was that it had to be big enough to really be useful on our farm here.

Over the years, Joanne would notice many small old Farmall

tractors that had been restored to like new condition and would think they were so cute! Of course, Joshua took a great interest in them too. My reply would be, "They're nice, but they're not for us because they're too small. You can hardly use them for anything on our farm."

Joshua agreed to my two conditions. Another thing was he wasn't ready to buy a tractor all by himself. I could well understand that. So after talking it over, we came to the agreement that we would each own fifty percent of the tractor. That made him really happy. He was very confident that I wouldn't buy a bad tractor or make a bad deal. It took a lot of pressure off of him.

So we started scanning the newspapers for a good tractor to buy. Every week we would check them along with all the auction bills. We came across a few possibilities that sounded good. When we came across one, I would immediately call the owner up and ask him a long list of questions I had concerning the tractor. Usually he would answer my questions assuring me that the tractor was in excellent shape – not a thing wrong with it. So with that, we would set up a time convenient for both of us to go and look at the "Perfect Tractor." Many times after looking at and test-running the tractor, we would leave, just shaking our heads in disbelief. Often times I said on the way home, "If the owner would have told me the truth about it when I talked to him on the phone, I would never even have went and looked at it."

To which my wife replied, "He knew that, and that's why he didn't tell you the truth."

One tractor we looked at was absolutely shocking. The owner had bought it off of a farmer in Iowa that had bought it brand new many years before. He assured us it was in super excellent condition, and we had better look at it soon before somebody else bought it from him. We went and looked at it and were shocked at what we saw. It had been stripped down and wasn't even safe to run. I did run it a little and it ran terrible. When I mentioned the condition of the tractor to the owner, he didn't think it was that bad. He did tell us though that his niece got killed by that tractor, but that didn't seem to affect him at all! We quickly told him, "No" and left. It is amazing what some people are like.

We went and looked at another tractor that was in "excellent shape." When we saw it, we were amazed at all the duct tape holding it together! I am not joking on this. The farmer assured me though that if I bought it, he would get it fixed up for me. I told him, "I don't think so" and left.

This was getting discouraging, trying to find a good used tractor to buy. Joshua really wanted one. I told him we had to have patience and in time we would get one. Patience can be hard to have when a boy has a bad case of tractor fever. I must say though, that Joshua did very well. Every time we looked at a tractor, afterwards we would talk it over, and I would always have him tell me first what he thought of it and why. This was very educational for Joshua, as well as for Catherine and Joanne. I would always tell them my opinion last. It was interesting; sometimes they would see stuff on the tractor that I would miss.

We were getting desperate to find a good used tractor. Finally, one day we stopped at our local implement shop and talked to the owner. Ron said he had a man from a fair distance away that wanted to trade his older Farmall in on a newer tractor that Ron had on his lot. He had pictures of it on the computer and it looked sharp! Needless to say, we were very interested. Through a lot of wheeling and dealing over the phone, we came to an agreement that was contingent on us looking at and running his tractor for final approval.

On the set day, Ron and I drove down to look at the tractor with plans to close the deal. Joshua had school that day, and so he couldn't go, but he gave me permission to buy the tractor if I thought it was a good deal. Ron and I checked it out, and it did pass muster. We were ready to close the deal when the owner told us he had to have $500 more than what we had agreed on. With that Ron got very upset and walked right out. I stayed a minute and questioned the man about the extra money, seeing we had already agreed on the price ahead of time. But he insisted he had to have $500 more. With that, I also in disgust went and joined Ron in the pickup and left.

On the way home, Ron and I talked quite a bit. We were both very upset with the man not keeping his word to us. I did ask Ron if he thought the tractor was worth $500 more. Ron thought on it a while and said, "I think you could buy it for that price and be O.K." That was kind of how I felt too, but both of us strongly disapproved of the owner breaking his word to us. I told Ron I would tell Joshua the whole story and let him decide.

When I got home later that day, Joshua was eagerly awaiting news on the tractor. I told him the whole story and his face went sad. I told him to think it over and decide. The next day he told me, "I don't want that tractor."

Later on when I told Ron, his reply was, "Fine, don't have him buy something he isn't going to feel good about."

With that I thanked Ron for both of us and said, "Good-bye."

It was getting so that I was hesitant to call on any more tractors. But shortly thereafter, we saw a different tractor advertised in the paper. I called on it, and the farmer made it sound like a really good one. So on a set Saturday, Joshua and I went and looked at it. Were we surprised; it looked decent and ran excellent. We agreed right there on it and bought the tractor from Ed. It's a Farmall 450 made in 1957. We have had it on our farm for a while now, and it has worked very well.

Looking back we are all very happy that we passed up all the previous tractors. Why did Joshua say no to the nice one that the farmer wanted $500 more for, you ask? It's a matter of integrity. We always taught our children early on to tell the truth and to keep their word. The Bible commands us parents, "Train up a child in the way he should go: and when he is old, he will not depart from it." So when the farmer wouldn't keep his word to us, Joshua wanted nothing to do with him. I couldn't blame him a bit, and I felt the same way.

So Joshua got cured of his tractor fever and learned a lot more about people. He also put in practice the principals we taught him from the Word of God. What's more than that, he saw God answer our prayers for a good used tractor.

Joshua by his tractor.

SIXTY-FIVE

Spring

After a long, cold, snowy winter, we greatly look forward to spring on the farm. It's nice to see the huge snow piles that have accumulated over the winter months melt away. Yes, there is lots of mud around and lots of work to do, but it's good to have the warm temperatures.

One of the first things we look forward to in the spring are the Canadian and snow-white Arctic geese flying north to Canada. It's great seeing their big V-shaped formations, flying over our buildings as they head straight north to their summer homes, honking and honking as they go. Sometimes they will land in our fields and scrounge up some food. Sometimes we will have hundreds or even thousands of them stop in to visit. We greatly enjoy having them, although they don't stay very long with spring in the air and Canada calling. When they leave, we always tell them, "Good-bye, we'll see you again in the fall."

And they always honk their "Good-byes" to us. It is truly amazing how the Creator, God, put it into these majestic birds to fly thousands of miles north every spring and then in the fall to travel thousands of miles south once again.

We also have a contest here every spring between the four of us. The contest is: who will see the first robin on our farm. The winner usually gets a special piece of candy, so needless to say we are all very attentive. We know with the robins back, spring is surely here.

Further into spring, the green grass starts to grow, especially next to the foundations of the buildings. The kids start to pick handfuls of this lush, juicy, green stuff and take them to the barn to give to their favorite cows. And the cows, what do they do? Out come their long tongues, twisting around the clumps of grass and quickly taking them in. In a matter of a few seconds, it's gone, and they're looking for more with their big bright eyes. This is always a very special treat for them.

Also with the green grass comes the beautiful spring flowers. The kids and I love to pick them and bring them into the house for Joanne. And she always greatly appreciates them – even if they are just dandelions at times.

With spring there is always so much new life. Part of every spring is Easter. Before I came to know Jesus as my personal Lord and Saviour, Easter was just another religious holiday. But once Jesus came into my heart, Easter took on a whole new meaning. The death, burial and resurrection of Jesus became very personal to me. With Jesus alive and living in my heart, He gave me life and that so much more abundantly. It was life like I had never experienced in all my growing up years! Before, life was so dead, hopeless and loveless, but now with Jesus it's just the opposite!

The Bible teaches that the creation declares the glory of God. I believe this is so true in the spring of the year when creation is all coming so alive.

So enjoy the geese, robins and all the flowers and be sure and give God thanks for it all. Spring shows us all that God sends new life every year. And the greatest part of spring was when Jesus came out of the grave to live forevermore. Because He lives, I live and you can too.

Do We Care About Our Fellow Man or Is It Just Money?

The milk we produce on our dairy farm here we sell to a farmer-owned and run cooperative that produces high quality cheese that is sold to customers all over the country. They have been in business for many years and have done an excellent job of producing and selling dairy products.

We have counted it a privilege to sell our milk there for many years. We always seek to take excellent care of our animals and to produce the highest quality milk possible. We say, "We have the privilege of producing high quality food to feed hungry people." As a matter of fact, we have won beautiful plaques over the years from the creamery for our exceptionally high quality milk.

The creamery, because of increased growth, is expanding to handle more milk. Part of that expansion is a new cheese store to better serve their ever-growing number of customers. I am in full support of the expansion, but I have a problem with one thing.

A couple months ago, I talked to the CEO of the creamery and asked him, "Once the new store is complete, will we be selling wine from it?"

He answered, "Yes."

This greatly disturbed my family and me. So a month ago, we went to the annual meeting, and I talked to the president of the board and expressed our concerns about this. He listened intently and then afterwards asked me if I would come the following week and address the board of directors about this issue, to which I agreed.

The creamery in its entire history has never sold alcohol. In recent years, the CEO has always been emphasizing to us farmers the importance of good public image. We need to take good care of our animals and the land that we farm. On our farm here, we look at our farm and the animals on it as a gift from God and always seek to take the very best care of it along with the animals. We have received many compliments over the years because of it.

I addressed the board on the alcohol issue and talked to them for a half hour. They were strongly in favor of selling it because from research done, it would increase cheese sales and profits. The point I brought up was caring for our customers and neighbors. I said, "For all the history of this creamery, it has not sold alcohol and has been very profitable. We have an excellent public image. What if somebody buys alcohol here and goes out drinking and driving and hurts or kills some innocent people? How would we feel about that and what would that do to the image of the creamery?"

Their response floored me. "We have liability insurance, we're protected."

From talking to the board president afterwards on the phone, it appears the board voted unanimously to approve the sale of alcohol in its new store. We as a family had been hoping and praying that they wouldn't sell it. We have seen so many accidents where people have been hurt, crippled or killed over the years because of alcohol. We have seen where a parent would go home drunk, and beat and abuse their family. The very ones they should care for and love the most. It has led to so many broken homes and marriages. So many innocent people getting hurt. No wonder the Bible says in Habakkuk 2:15, "Woe unto him that giveth his neighbor drink, that puttest thy bottle to him, and makest him drunken also."

We as a family would much rather receive a little less money from the creamery and not have them sell alcohol. I emphasized to the board the terrible things alcohol is responsible for, and yet they voted for it so they could make more money. Money was what mattered. Not the people who would be hurt and killed by it. No wonder the Bible says, "The love of money is the root of all evil."

We as a family care for our neighbors and customers who buy our dairy products. We wish our creamery did too, but unfortunately that is not the case. Now we are left wondering, "Where do we sell our milk in the future?"

SIXTY-SEVEN

A Sleepless Night

A number of years ago, when I had a silo built here, a very interesting thing happened. Something I'm not pleased about at all, but rather ashamed of. I share it with you though, hoping you can learn from my mistake.

In this particular situation, the crew of men that built my silo had several more silos to build after they finished mine. So needless to say, they were in a hurry to get my silo done, so they could move on to the next job. Once they had my silo done, they moved on to the next job, leaving a mess of broken concrete staves and metal behind.

We as a family were so glad to have our new silo done that we joyfully went to work cleaning up the mess they left behind. In the process of cleaning it up, we found a very expensive, name brand ratchet they had left behind. They had thrown it away because it had broken.

I eyed it up because I knew that tool company had a lifetime warranty on all its tools. Their tools were premium quality and carried a premium price tag. Thus, I had never bought a single tool from them, but I had admired their line of tools for years. Now, here I had one of their ratchets with a lifetime warranty on it. I use ratchets with sockets a lot on the farm here fixing machinery.

Once we had the mess cleaned up, I called around to find a store that carried that brand of tools. A couple days later, I took it into the store and showed it to the man behind the counter. He looked it over and replied, "No problem, I'll give it to the company man when he comes around next week, and then you can come in and get a brand new ratchet free."

I thanked him and left with a big smile on my face. Boy, was I looking forward to this expensive, top of the line ratchet. What a deal! But down inside I didn't feel quite right about it. I brushed off those inner feelings though and went about the rest of my day.

I went to bed that night and fell asleep fast, but then shortly after that, I woke up and couldn't get back to sleep. I tossed and turned for hours. Down inside I knew what was wrong. The lifetime warranty was for the owner of the tool. I had never bought it, and the rightful owners had thrown it away. It was wrong for me to try and claim their warranty. In doing so, I would really be stealing from the company. Right there, lying in bed, I repented of my sin and asked the Lord to forgive me. And He did, and then I went back to sleep until my alarm clock went off.

After doing morning chores, I called the store up and talked to the man behind the counter again. I told him exactly what happened and apologized for being deceitful.

His response, "That's all right, people do that all the time here."

I replied, "It's not all right, it's stealing and I was wrong."

With that he absolutely insisted that I take the new ratchet because people do it all the time. Nobody would know the difference.

I strongly replied, "I'll know the difference and so will God. I'm not going to lose anymore sleep over a ratchet!"

He was flabbergasted and said, "What should I do with this busted ratchet then?"

I responded, "Throw it in the garbage; I don't ever want to see that thing again!" With that we said, "Good-bye."

Needless to say, I slept really well the next night. It is always right to be honest. Human nature always wants a good deal. We must always be careful that that doesn't lead us into sin. In the years since then, I've always been glad that I did the honest thing. If I wouldn't have done it, I would always have regretted it. I would have never enjoyed using that tool either. And it isn't worth sleepless nights and a broken relationship with God. That would be terrible.

SIXTY-EIGHT

One of Those Days

We all have days once in a while where it seems if something can go wrong it does. And it just isn't one thing that goes wrong; it seems that they just pile up! I had one day like that a while back here. We were starting to cut a new crop of hay on this particular day. I had my 1206 Farmall tractor sitting in the shed in front of the tractor that I had my discbine hooked up to. The plan was to drive the old dependable 1206 out of the shed and put it on the blower for filling the silo with the hay I was about to cut. The tractor started right up, and I drove it out of the shed and turned it to head to the silo. I was turning it right in the middle of our drive way when I saw that the front wheel was almost ready to fall off. I quickly pushed in the clutch and stopped. In my many years of running tractors, I never had anything like this happen.

My kids came to see why I had stopped the tractor right in the middle of the driveway. We were all shocked to see the wheel almost ready to fall off. Joshua asked me, "What do we do?"

I replied, "We have to get it fixed so that we can move it out of the way; our milk hauler can't even get up to the milk house to get our milk." With that we went and got a bunch of tools out of our shop and went to work on it. The inside wheel bearing was chewed up into an innumerable number of pieces. The outside wheel bearing was still good. By running the tractor like this over time, it had put a lot of pressure on the pack nut holding the wheel on. Over time, the threads on the spindle which hold the pack nut on stripped half off. Then the cotter pin that goes through the pack nut and spindle sheared off. The end result was my wheel falling almost off on this particular day. On this day when I really wanted to go at haying! Surprisingly the tractor had run really nice with the inner wheel bearing out until this day.

Once we had it apart, I headed for the phone to call my local machine shops to see if they had the bearing I needed. To my astonishment, they didn't have it. I turned to my family and said, "What do we do? We can't go at haying with the tractor setting there, and our milk hauler can't even get in here to get the milk." With that we started to pray for wisdom in what to do. With that an idea came to my mind. Our neighbors up the road have a large front-end loader, so I decided to call them and see if they could bring it down and lift the front end of my tractor up and push it out of the way. I figured we could fix it later on after haying. The idea would have probably worked, but my neighbors were gone for the day.

So we were back to square one again, what do we do? Joanne kept praying while I started to make more phone calls. I finally located a bearing a fair distance away. I wanted to replace both bearings, but they only had the inner one. I asked him to hold it for me, and with that we got into the car and went after it.

Back home, we put the new bearing in and the used outer bearing. We greased them and tightened up the packing nut. But the packing nut wouldn't tighten up; it just started to jump the damaged threads on the spindle. Now what do we do? It seemed like it was impossible to get it fixed and out of the way.

I said to my family, "This is going to take a lot to get this fixed right, and we don't have the time or stuff here now to do it."

Catherine said, "Yes, but what do we do with this tractor in the middle of the driveway?"

I replied, "We'll put a new cotter pin through the packing nut and spindle. I think with those two bearings in the wheel and the pack nut on loosely, I can real slowly back it into the corner of the shed and park it there till we have time after haying to fix it right." And that's what we did.

By now it was late afternoon, and I finally headed out to the hayfield just west of the barn. Was I ever happy to be finally cutting hay! The rest of my family headed to the barn to clean the gutters. I was just making my second round around the outside of the field when Catherine came walking out. On this particular day, I figured she wasn't bringing good news. She told me the barn cleaner had broken. So, I stopped the tractor and headed for the barn. It took a little bit, but we got it fixed and running good again. I headed back to the hayfield and started to cut hay again. By this time it was getting really late in the day, and I ended up cutting just a few acres of hay.

It was time to get at the evening chores and to our surprise we had a real sick cow. I wasn't expecting this at all, but a lot of the previous stuff in the day I hadn't expected either. We ended up giving her an IV in her neck and praying for her. If we couldn't pray, I don't know what we would do! I'm so glad to have a heavenly Father that answers our prayers. Well, we got our evening chores all done and called it a day.

Fortunately, the following days went a lot better, and we got our hay all off. The barn cleaner kept working well, and our cow recovered. In time we got our 1206 fixed and running again.

Even though that day didn't go at all as planned, we still had a good day working together as a family. We've learned no matter what comes our way, if we look to the Lord and rule our spirits, we can and will overcome our adversities.

SIXTY-NINE

It All Started So Innocently

When I was a teenager, I would oftentimes spend a couple weeks every summer helping my uncle George and my grandmother on their dairy farm. I so looked forward to those couple weeks all year long when I could go live with them and work alongside George. It was the highlight of my year, since my home life wasn't that good.

My uncle George and Grandma treated me wonderfully. I would work alongside George from early morning till late at night. Whether it was milking cows, grinding feed, putting up hay, cleaning calf pens, or the many other jobs there were to do, he was always great to work with.

One early summer day, something happened that affected my life for years afterwards. On that particular day, we baled our first field of hay for the season. After taking the first crop of hay off of that field that day, George wanted to work the field and plant it to corn. He figured it was early enough in the season so that he could get a good crop of corn off of it come fall.

So after we had the hay baled that day, George hooked the tractor up to the disk and told me to go out and disk that field. As I headed out to the field, he went to the barn to get ready for the evening milking. I started disking the field, and everything was going great until something broke on the tractor's hitch. I got off the tractor and looked it over and saw two possible ways to fix it. I wasn't sure which way to do it, and since it wasn't mine, I figured I'd better go in and ask George how he wanted it done.

Since it was only about a hundred yards north of the barn, I decided I might as well walk in instead of driving the equipment in. I found George in the milk house with his back towards the door. He jumped when I opened the door and walked in. He quickly turned and faced me while hiding something behind his back. I was extremely interested in what he had behind his back because I'd never seen him act this way before. He wanted to know what I wanted, and so I told him about the tractor. Then I asked him what he was hiding. It was clear to him that he couldn't really hide it on me, so he pulled it out from behind his back. It was his latest issue of *Playboy* magazine. I was shocked. I had never seen one before. Now here my uncle that I thought so highly of was holding one in his hands. He said, "It's only this, just a little fun entertainment." Then he said, "We'd better go and get that tractor fixed so you can finish disking that field this evening yet."

With that we headed out to the field and fixed the tractor. A couple hours later, I finished disking the field and drove into the farm yard. I saw George working in the barn so I went to help him. He had a big surprise waiting for me. He had laid out a whole pile of his magazines for me to look at. I knew it was wrong so I pretty much avoided them, but later that evening he showed me a bunch of the pictures in them that he really liked. With that, he got me looking at them. Up until that day, I never knew that George was into pornography.

I must say that George never mistreated me. But after that day, I started to look at his pornography and started to enjoy it. The more I looked at it, the more I enjoyed it. Every time I went to stay with him, I'd find myself looking at it. The Bible is most certainly right when it teaches in Hebrews 11:25 that there is pleasure in sin for a season.

Did it hurt me at all, you ask? Absolutely yes! The more I looked at it, the more I started to look down on women. The more perverted thoughts ran through my mind. I've read accounts over the years of men that started looking at porn for pleasure, and eventually they ended up assaulting women and in some cases killing them. How tragic!

Although I never assaulted or killed a woman, I most certainly did not treat them with the respect I should have. Fortunately, when I was twenty years old, I repented of my sins, including pornography, and accepted Jesus as my Lord. He saved me then, and as I started to follow Him, He began to deal with me in my attitudes towards women. Boy, did I need that. As I look back, I am amazed at how perverted my mind was regarding women.

Thank God for His Word! For through His Word my mind got straightened out. Seven years later, I was blessed to marry a beautiful, godly woman – Joanne. I've had the privilege of being married to her for over twenty years now and having a wonderful family.

I got caught up into porn so innocently, and because of my sinful nature, I became a slave to it. But, by the power of God I've been set free. So many men, women and children are affected by porn today in our society. It destroys families, marriages and individuals. The toll is terrible. And it just isn't in magazines anymore. It's all around us today – on TV, computers, billboards and so forth. Is it any wonder that there are so many abortions today and rapes and people in prison?

Looking back, I wish I had never got caught up into porn, but I thank the Lord for forgiveness and for setting me on the right path. The years after I got saved have most definitely been the best years of my life. If I would have continued in my sin,

I definitely would not be where I am today. The Bible says it well when it says in John 10:10, "The thief cometh not, but for to steal, and to kill, and to destroy: I am come that they might have life, and that they might have it more abundantly."

Just a little fun entertainment? Definitely not! Deadly destroying entertainment? Yes, a thousand times over.

If you are caught up in porn, I know a Saviour who loves you and wants to forgive you and set you free. The choice is yours. I have never regretted following Him, I just wish I would have done it sooner.

The Two-Dollar Wheelbarrow

Many years ago, shortly after we bought our farm, I went to a farm auction that had lots of stuff for sale by a farmer who was retiring. One of the things that came up for sale was his old wheelbarrow. It was a heavy-duty one that had been welded up some, leaked in the corners, but was still in good solid working condition. I knew I could sure use it on my farm. The auctioneer opened up the bidding on it for one dollar and immediately somebody said, "Yes." Then he asked for two dollars and I raised my hand. Then he asked for three dollars and I held my breath. To my amazement, nobody raised my bid so the auctioneer said, "Sold." I had just bought a two-dollar wheelbarrow.

Over the last twenty-two years, we have used it for lots of work on our farm here. From hauling dirt and rock, to hay bales and feed, we have used it for a tremendous amount of work. I've done a little bit of welding on it over the years, but pretty much it's been trouble free.

This last spring, I had to replace some of the old bolts and washers holding the thing together with new ones. I told the kids then that we could buy a new one and that I was sure we had gotten our two dollars' worth of use out of it. "But, Dad," they said, "Why spend all that money on a new one when we can fix up 'Old Dependable'?" Well, it's hard to argue with my kids, especially when I'm of the same mind-set that they are, so we fixed it up.

A month later, Joshua was hauling a load of shale rock with it that weighed between two and three hundred pounds when the wheel rim bent sideways. Considering it is probably forty to fifty years old and fairly rusty, it's not surprising. Actually, it's surprising it made it this long. We were all disappointed to see it. I told the kids, "It's definitely time to buy a new one now."

Their reply, "But can't we fix it up some way?"

I told them, "I don't think so; it's time for a new one." Needless to say their faces were down cast.

A few days later we went to a store that sells wheelbarrows. I had my mind made up that we were going to buy a new one. They had several on display, but we were greatly disappointed as we looked at them. They were all built so cheap and light. I said to my family, "They will never stand up to the work we have for them on our farm. I'm not buying one of these." The kids agreed with me.

Joanne said, "What are we going to do then?"

I answered, "I don't know, but I'm not buying one of these that's built so cheap, it won't last."

So with that we continued walking through the store and came to a place where they sold wheelbarrow tires. I thought, "Here's our answer." They cost thirty to forty some dollars. I told the kids that that was a lot to stick into a two-dollar wheelbarrow. But they thought it was worth saving. But, as we looked at them, we saw that the rims were built so light that they would never stand up to the loads we put in our wheelbarrow. So again I said, "No." I left the store in frustration. It's sad that sometimes in America today, it's impossible to buy a quality built item.

Later that day, Joshua came up to me and said, "Could we

use an old steel wheel off of the chopper hay head that we've got junked-out up in the woods?"

I thought on it a minute and said, "It might work." Needless to say, we were desperate to find an answer to our problem. Well, we went up there, and after a fair bit of work we got both steel wheels off of the old junked-out hay head.

We got them and the old wheelbarrow in the shop and went to work. The kids were very eager to help me since they didn't want to see Old Dependable junked out. They thought I was going to put one steel wheel on it, but I said, "Why not put both of them on it?" So that's what we did. A couple hours later we rolled Old Dependable out of the shop. It looks like we're going backwards in time since it originally came out with a rubber tire and now it has two steel wheels on it.

Since then we've used it a lot, and it has worked great. I told the kids that we spent about two dollars on new nuts, bolts and washers for it, so it had better go another twenty-two years so that I get my money out of it! They laughed and agreed. Looking at it, we think it might make another twenty-two years. I'm sure it will go a lot further than one of those new ones that we looked at.

Sometimes it's hard to throw old things away that have special memories with them. The kids think it's pretty special that the two-dollar wheelbarrow we started farming with years ago is still working. It's hard for us to throw stuff away that has worked well over the years if it's possible to fix it up and keep it working.

And what is more amazing and special is that God loves to take broken, hopeless people and rescue them and then fix them up and use them for His glory. That's what the gospel is all about. I know this is true because I'm one of those that He's saved. The wonderful news is that He will save anybody who cries out to Him. He never throws anybody away.

Our steel wheeled wheelbarrow.

SEVENTY-ONE

A Dirty Thankless Job

Every year in the fall we have our neighbors, Howard and his son Bob, come and combine our corn. As one of them drives their large machine down the rows of corn, it snaps the ears from the stalks. Then it takes the ears into the heart of the machine where it shells the kernels off of the cobs and augers them up into the grain tank. From there, it gets loaded onto a truck and hauled into my farmyard here where we run it through a roller mill. The mill breaks up the kernels and blows them up into our silo. By processing our corn this way, it makes it highly digestible for our cattle. With our small silo full of corn, we have enough grain to feed our cattle for another year.

But, harvest isn't over yet. The grain is off, but the rest of the corn plant is still in the field. This also is very valuable to us. We use this to bed our cattle with over the long cold winter months. It is very soft, absorbent, and helps to keep our cattle warm and comfortable. We call it "cornstalk bedding."

So, after the corn is combined, I take a tractor and flail chopper out to the field and run the cornstalks through the chopper. It cuts the stalks, leaves and husks into small pieces and blows them back onto the ground. This is necessary because the stalks have a lot of juice in them. By doing this, it helps them to dry out. If cornstalks get put up with too much moisture in them, they will mold and possibly catch on fire. After we have them chopped, we leave them lay for a few days to dry.

Then it's time to harvest them. I rake them into large rolls with our rotary rake. Then I take the tractor with the same flail chopper back to the field; this time though, I have a large chopper box hooked behind it. I head the chopper down the large roll, chopping it into the chopper box. Because the cornstalks are dry and since the rake put a little bit of dry soil in with them, my flail chopper puts up a large cloud of dust. It's unavoidable.

Once I have the chopper box full, I take it home and unload it into an elevator that takes it up into the barn where we store it. Unloading the bedding into the elevator is also a very dirty, dusty job. Joanne, Catherine and Joshua are in the mow moving all this and packing it away while I'm unloading it. By the end of the day, we all look like we've been in a terrible dust storm! We all wear glasses and masks to keep the dirt out of our eyes and noses. It usually takes us a full week to put our bedding all up.

I remember one day after I had unloaded several loads of very dusty bedding and was in the process of finishing up another one, a lady walked up behind me. Since I was almost done, I finished unloading it while she stood about fifty feet away. When I got done, I walked over to see what she wanted. The first words out of her mouth were, "That's sure a dirty thankless job." Then she went on to tell me that in her previous marriage she had helped her husband put up cornstalk bedding. She had hated it because of how dirty it was.

I was shocked at her comments and attitude. While it is a very dirty job, the four of us here have always enjoyed doing it. It's very rewarding seeing the barn full of soft fluffy bedding at the end of the harvest season. We use this bedding every day throughout the next year for our cattle. The cattle sure appreciate it and do well on it. When we see our cattle lying in it very contentedly and even mooing occasionally, we know they appreciate it, even if they can't say it in English! A dirty thankless job – we don't think so. A dirty job, yes; a thankless job, no!

It is so important for a person in their work to keep a good attitude. If you keep a good attitude, your work will be much more enjoyable and rewarding. If you don't, your work will be miserable, and the hours will just drag by. The same can be said for marriage, family and so many other things too.

I know there are many people who do ordinary jobs where they receive very little thanks or appreciation. Sometimes they wonder if it's really worth it. Let me tell you something, if you are doing a service to others and blessing them, it most certainly is worth it. The Bible says in Galatians 6:9, "Let us not be weary in well doing: for in due season we shall reap if we faint not."

I've never heard my bossie cows say, "Thank you" in English yet, but I know they sure appreciate us putting up all that dry fluffy cornstalk bedding. It's too bad that lady didn't hear her cows saying, "Thank you" years before. If she would have, I'm sure she would have enjoyed her work much more and found it rewarding. I know we do here.

Tom chopping cornstalk bedding.

Mom

There was a very special little girl born on November 6, 1927, in a farmhouse five miles west of Augusta, Wisconsin. For her parents, George and Augusta Elbert, this was their third and final child. They realized children are a gift from God and that every life is of great value. So they sought to train up their children: Alice, George and Ruth according to the Bible.

Ruth, my mother, walked with her brother and sister to a one-room country school house which was over two miles from home. The school had just one teacher who taught all eight grades. The teacher got paid very little, but she was excellent and very thankful to have a job during the Great Depression. Mom loved school and was a very bright and diligent student.

One day when Mom was six or seven years old, something happened at school that changed her life forever. An adult, whom my mother did not know, came to school one day and with the teacher's blessing, and also that of the school board, spoke to all the students.

He opened up his Bible and read a number of verses out of it to the students. He told them that they were sinners going to hell, but that God loved them so much He didn't want them to go to hell. So He sent His only Son, Jesus, to die a horrible death on a cross to pay for all of their sins so that they could go to heaven. He told them the way to receive this great gift from God was to ask God to forgive them of their sins, then to ask Jesus to come and live in their hearts and commit to live for Him and follow Him all the days of their lives. He then led the class in a prayer doing that. My mother told me years later, when I told her how I got born again, that she bowed her head that day and asked Jesus into her heart and committed to live for Him and follow Him all the rest of her days.

Mom was not a house girl. She told me many times over the years that she would much rather be outside helping her dad and brother than to work in the house with her mother. She greatly enjoyed helping them get the crops in and taking care of all the cattle. Whether it was putting up the hay for the cattle, or helping to milk the cows by hand, or feeding the calves, or taking care of the chickens, Mom was there always helping them out.

Mom graduated from high school and got a job in Eau Claire. But, she just couldn't sit there on the weekends. She had to get back to the farm. So every Friday night, her dad would drive twenty-five miles to Eau Claire and bring her back home to the farm. Then on Sunday night, he would take her back for the week.

During her growing-up years, her parents had struggled greatly financially. So when Mom got a job, she finally had money of her own to spend on things she wanted. What were they, you ask? One thing was her own personal Bible with lots of study notes. That extra-large, very thick Bible would be extremely precious to her all the rest of her life.

After a number of years, my mother met my dad who was farming, and eventually they got married. They were both very hard workers, and so the farm prospered. They were blessed with four children. Mom told me years later, when she was pregnant the first time that she was so hoping and praying that she would have a girl. Her hope came true, and she had Judy. Next she had two sons, Paul and Karl. When she was pregnant the fourth time, she knew that that would be her last child because of health issues. She was very happy with the three children she already had, but this time she wanted one more daughter to balance the family out. Well, she got me, Tom, the one who writes these stories. Sometimes we don't always get what we hope for!

Unfortunately, life doesn't always go smoothly and nice. Sometimes it gets very hard and difficult. Such was the case for Mom after she got married. But, what saw her through it all was her faith in God. I clearly remember that she would get up every morning a little after 4 a.m. and read a devotional and, yes, her very large Bible. I know she told me a couple of times over the years when life was very difficult for me that she prayed for us four children every single morning during her Bible time.

It was that Bible time every morning with her Lord that saw her through all the hard years.

On October 24, I stopped and saw Mom at the nursing home for the last time. This time I told her again how I loved her and appreciated all she had done for us over the years. I read my Bible to her and prayed with her a number of times. I wanted to make sure that she was ready to see Jesus. And then I said good-bye to her, knowing very well that I might not see her alive again on this side. Three days later, Mom passed from this life.

Mom was not perfect by any means; she had her faults and shortcomings. But it was for sinners that Jesus came into the world.

It doesn't matter how good or how bad of a life you've lived. I know a Saviour who came from glory to die for a world of lost sinners. You need to tell Him you are truly sorry for all of your sins and willing to change your ways and follow Him. Then ask Him to come into your heart and be your Lord and Saviour. He will give you a life that is truly worth living and a home in heaven afterwards.

Mom is gone now, and I will surely miss her, but I believe I will see her again.

SEVENTY-THREE

Christmas During the Great Depression

The older I get, the more it seems that I look back at past Christmases. The one thing that really stands out in my memory is my mother telling me a number of times about her childhood Christmases during the Great Depression. I guess the reason I really remember them is because they were so different from what is normal in America today.

Mom's parents back then farmed their 160 acre farm, along with some rented acreage, five miles west of Augusta, Wisconsin. Back then they used horses to work the land and to put up the crops. So they always had several horses on the farm along with some dairy cows. They also raised hogs and chickens. They had a very diversified farming operation. They sold milk, meat, eggs and crops from their farm.

The problem back then was that prices for farm commodities were extremely low, so it was almost impossible for them to make a profit on the farm, even though they were very hard workers. Added to that was the fact that during the 1930s they had many years of severe drought, so they didn't get much for crops. If all of this wasn't bad enough, they had a double mortgage on the farm. They lived for years under the constant threat that the bank would foreclose on them.

So what did my mom and her sister and brother get for Christmas a lot of those years, you ask? The answer will probably shock you, but it is the truth. Just before Christmas, Mom's dad would go into town and buy three oranges. On Christmas Day, each child got one orange to eat. It was the only time of year that they ever got an orange to eat! And how they savored them; they were such a special treat, and they knew their parents had sacrificed to buy them.

Is that all they got, you ask? Well, yes and no. That's all their parents could afford to buy them. But they got so much more. They had godly parents who loved them greatly. They read the Bible to them and told them of God's great gift to man. How God's Son, Jesus, was born in an animal stable to a very poor couple many years ago to save all of us from our sins. They told them that that was the whole meaning of Christmas.

On Christmas Day, Mom's dad would hook a horse up to the sleigh and take his family to church where the children participated in a special children's program. The preacher would once again read Luke 2:1-20 and tell of the greatest gift ever given to mankind – Jesus.

My mom told me this many times over the years. Not because of how hard those Christmases were, but because of how blessed they were.

Today, in our society, so much is made of buying piles of gifts to put under the Christmas tree. But, all those gifts don't really buy happiness. True happiness comes from receiving God's great gift, Jesus, into our hearts. Once you have Jesus in your heart, then you know what Christmas is all about.

If you have Jesus in your heart and the love of God in your home, as my mom did, you are truly blessed. She was and she knew it, even if there were only three oranges under their Christmas tree!

SEVENTY-FOUR

A Good Example

When we bought our farm here many years ago, we were pleased to see that there was a wood furnace in the basement of the house. Buying this farm put us deeply in debt, so we were glad that we could heat our house with firewood instead of costly fuel. So over all these years, I've never bought a drop of fuel to heat our home with. Instead it's been all firewood – and lots of it.

Over time, the furnace in the basement came to the end of its useful life. Since we enjoy a nice cozy house in the wintertime to come into after doing chores out in the cold, the decision to stay with wood heat was an easy one to make. This time though, we bought an outdoor wood furnace to heat our home with. In time we named it "Little Smokie." I like having the fire and firewood outside; it's a lot safer and less work to keep going. I also like the fact that I don't have to get up at 2 a.m. on bitter cold nights to reload the furnace. Our outdoor one holds enough wood to keep it going all night long. Another plus with this is that we heat all of our house and milk house hot water with it which really helps save money. At times we even take hot water from the milk house to melt the ice in our cattle's water tanks.

So doing all this with Little Smokie requires a lot of firewood.

But that's no problem; we have a big woods on our farm, and we enjoy making firewood. Every year late in the fall, Catherine, Joshua and I head down to the woods to cut trees for firewood. First we try to cut the trees that have died recently and those that have gone down due to storms. After that, we tend to cut trees along the edges of our fields.

It's very peaceful working in the woods in the fall of the year. Often times we see deer, squirrels, chipmunks, raccoons and other wildlife out there. Also, we see many birds out there, including large flocks of geese flying overhead telling us that winter is on the way.

But, working out there with large trees and chainsaws can be dangerous too. Sometimes a tree doesn't fall the way a person thinks it will. So when falling a tree, a person needs to be extremely careful.

A while back, I decided to cut a large maple tree down that was on the edge of my cornfield. I looked it over carefully and decided that it would want to fall to the north. So I cut a small wedge out of the north side of it and then started cutting through from the south side. Well, I got almost through, and then the tree instead of falling to the north came back and pinched my chainsaw tight.

I knew I was in a dangerous situation. I looked it over carefully and prayed for wisdom. I decided the best thing to do would be to get the five log chains that I had on the tractor that I drove to the woods that day, hook them to the tree, and pull it to the north.

I've always told my helpers to always keep their eyes on a tree that's been partially cut when working around it because there is always the chance it could go down unexpectedly. People have gotten hurt and sometimes killed in such situations.

So when my chainsaw got stuck, I asked Joshua to bring a log chain and put it on the north side of the tree, reminding him to keep an eye on the tree at all times. He got the first chain and put it there while I went after a second one. I was putting my chain on the north side of the tree and following my own advice – keeping my eyes on the tree at all times. It's a good thing that I was! As I was about to put my chain down, a small breeze picked up out of the south. The large maple tree started to come straight north. Immediately, I dropped my chain, stepped back and to the side of the tree trunk, grabbed my chainsaw, which was now free, and pulled it out. The tree crashed down right on top of the chain that I had just dropped on the ground seconds earlier! If I hadn't followed my own advice and kept my eyes on the tree, I would have been killed! The way it was, we were all perfectly safe, and we gave thanks to God.

I have always sought to give my children good advice and to follow the advice I give them. Too many times parents tell their kids, "Do as I say and not as I do." Many children do as their parents do and end up ruining their lives. Parents need to realize that their actions speak a lot louder than their words. But, when their actions line up with their words, they leave a powerful lasting impression on their children's lives. The Bible says, "Train up a child in the way he should go: and when he is old, he will not depart from it." This is most certainly true, but we must realize that we need to live rightly before them every day ourselves. Then we can expect them to listen to us, follow our example, and be blessed. If we do this, we also will be truly blessed. I know I am; the big maple tree crashing to the ground didn't hurt me a bit.

Tom falling a tree.

SEVENTY-FIVE

Don't Believe Everything You Hear

About fifteen years ago, I bought a new box manure spreader to use on our farm. It worked excellently over the years, needing only minor repairs. I was pleased with it even if it took a little bit of work to clean it up good every day in the winter to keep it running well. It had to be cleaned up well in freezing weather, or else it would freeze up and break down. I have to have my spreader working every day to clean my dairy barn.

Well, this last spring, after many years of faithful service, it was starting to have some major problems. So instead of starting to spend a lot of money fixing it up, we decided it was time to look for a new one. I had heard some people really brag up a different type of spreader called a slinger. Its design is totally different from my old box spreader. I never had any experience with one before, but I was open to checking one out.

I went to a machinery dealership that sold them and talked to the salesman. I had a number of questions for him regarding the spreader. But, I had one really big question for him regarding how the spreader would work in the wintertime. How much cleanup would it take to keep it running and not freezing up? He told me the spreader didn't need any cleanup at all except a little bit on the discharge chute which would only take a couple minutes. It sounded too good to be true, but the more I questioned him on it, the more he absolutely insisted it was true. He said, "Once in a while it will freeze up a little bit in the spreader, but then all you have to do is leave the spreader set out in the sun or put a heater in it for a little while."

I really liked the idea of faster and easier cleanup and less maintenance than what a box spreader required. So with his assurances that it would work super well in the winter time, I wrote out a check and bought one.

Well, winter came, and all of his assurances froze up! The spreader froze up terribly bad and broke down a number of times. On a number of days, Joshua and I would have to take an ax and big iron bar to chop the frozen material in the spreader to get it going. Sometimes we would spray a lot of hot water in it to get it to go. Needless to say, it broke down a number of times, and we had to fix on it to get it going again. I'm so thankful that my family helped me so much with it.

Finally, with it broke down and froze up really bad, I called up the dealership that sold it to me and told them what was happening with it. The owner acted real surprised, but he wouldn't send anybody out to look at it or help me out. I then called my local implement shop and asked them if I could put my spreader in their heated shop overnight. I was so blessed that they said yes. Actually, they let me have it in there for twenty-four hours. And it is amazing, even after twenty-four hours, Joshua and I worked for nearly an hour to get the frozen material all busted up and free inside the spreader. So much for not freezing up or only needing a little heat to thaw it out!

About the time we were ready to leave the implement shop, an employee named Fred walked through and talked to us. He told us, "We get a number of those spreaders in here every winter to thaw out. They freeze up bad." With that, I fully realized that the salesman from the other implement shop had not been honest with me. Also, that's why the owner of the implement shop wouldn't help us out at all when we were having so many troubles with it.

Back on the farm with it, I started to take a stepladder to the field every day so I could clean it up good on the inside so it wouldn't freeze up again and break down. That did work, but it was dangerous doing it. We finally decided it wasn't worth the risk and all the work that it took. We decided to trade it in and buy a new box spreader.

I called up Dale at my local implement shop where I had gotten my spreader thawed out and told him what I wanted. I was blessed in that he had just the right size box spreader on hand for me. I told him I wanted to trade my slinger in on it. So a couple days later he came out and looked at it and said, "I could live with $2,500 to boot."

I thought on it a few seconds and said, "I can live with that too." With that I reached out my hand and he shook it.

A couple days later, they brought out my new spreader and took my old spreader away. Boy, was I glad to see it go down the road! Our new spreader works super well and is so much easier and safer to clean up.

Shortly after getting our new box spreader, I had it sitting up by the barn one day when Craig, our milk truck driver, came. He said, "You got a new spreader; you had a slinger didn't you?"

To which I replied, "Yes, but it was freezing up so bad that I got rid of it."

To which Craig answered, "Yes, I know a lot of farmers with that type of spreader that have them freeze up bad. There's no way to keep them from doing that."

With that Craig left, and I stood there thinking, "I wish I would have talked to him about slinger spreaders before I bought the one that I did."

The slinger spreader I bought sounded almost too good to be true, and it was. It's too bad that the salesman wasn't truthful about it. In our world today, salesmen, politicians and many others will lie to us or try to deceive us for their own benefit. We have to be extremely careful and not believe everything we hear.

But there is One Who never lies to us or seeks to deceive us. He is God. He has made us an offer that is too good to be true, and yet it is true. He gave His Son, Jesus, to pay the price for our sins to redeem us. If we will repent of our sins and ask Jesus to be the Lord of our lives, He will forgive us, save us, and give us the best lives possible. I know this is most certainly true from experience. Even though my slinger spreader did not live up to expectations, Jesus always lives up to my best expectations and exceeds them. What a deal!

Tom by his new box spreader.

SEVENTY-SIX

An Unwanted Family

This last summer we had a family move in here unexpectedly. They never asked us if they could come and live here or not. They just set up their home out by my silos. One day Joshua was mowing the grass out there, and he spotted four of them. They were as surprised to see him as he was to see them. He immediately came running to the house to tell the rest of us about them. I quickly grabbed my gun and went running out there, but by the time I got there, they had disappeared. Needless to say, I was disappointed. I had hoped that I could shoot them and get rid of them.

What sort of a family was this that I wanted to shoot them on sight, you ask? A family of skunks! I started to look around and quickly found a freshly dug hole going down between my silo and the corner of my silo room. It was obvious that this new family of skunks had set up housekeeping there. The kids asked me, "What do we do now?"

I replied, "We have to get them out of here; it isn't safe for us or our cattle to have them around."

What makes skunks so dangerous on a dairy farm, you ask? Rabies. Skunks love milk, so they will hang around dairy cows that are outside at night and try to nurse on them. Often times in doing that, they will bite the cow lightly, and that is all it takes to transmit the rabies virus. The cow that gets rabies will die a very horrible death after several months. Since farmers work with cows, it's easy for farmers to catch the virus. All it takes is a little saliva from an infected cow getting into a little nick or scratch on a farmer's hand, and he will have it too.

If this happens to a farmer, he has to get a lot of very painful shots from a doctor so that he doesn't die. I know personally of a farm couple that had this happen to them years ago. Cheryl said, "The shots were terrible, and you never want to go through that!" She also told me one other interesting fact that shocked me. "Skunks will not die from rabies; they're the only animal that it doesn't kill."

So, knowing all this, I had no tolerance for a family of skunks around my barn. The question the kids asked was, "How do we get rid of them?"

I said, "I don't want to set a trap now since we are going at putting up a new crop of hay. Let's keep our eyes open; hopefully in the coming days we can see them outside here and shoot them." It sounded like a good plan, but it never worked that way. Yes, we did see them outside a number of times, but by the time we got the gun, they were gone.

Well, we got our hay put up, and I knew we had to try a different approach. I decided to set a large cage trap for them just a few feet in front of their hole. So, the kids and I set it using some broken ice cream cones and cookies as bait. Then we prayed, asking the Lord to bless it and help us catch the skunks.

Needless to say, when we went to bed that night, we were all excited to see what our trap would have in it the next morning. And were we ever surprised when we got out there the next morning and saw what we had! We had our big cat, Mr. Stripey, caught in the trap with his tail straight up and all his hair standing on end. He was spatting and putting out a ferocious growl. A large skunk was just a few feet away from him with its tail up in the air aiming right for him. Mr. Stripey, being in the cage trap, couldn't get away from the skunk and he was terrified. I don't blame him. The skunk was scared of the cat that was between him and his hole. The skunk knew he had to get into his hole for safety, which meant he had to pass within eighteen inches of a growling Mr. Stripey! I felt sorry for our cat; I thought for sure he was going to get sprayed by the skunk at extremely close range.

Once again I got my gun and ran with it. I wanted to do all I could to spare Mr. Stripey from a terrible experience. When I got back, I was surprised to find out that the skunk had gotten its courage up, walked by our cat, and went down in its hole without spraying him. I was relieved that our cat didn't get sprayed, but was disappointed that I still hadn't gotten rid of any of the skunks. I opened up the trap, and Mr. Stripey set a world's speed record for getting out of there! I never saw a cat go so fast in my life.

Well, I was back to square one. I had a whole family of skunks living under my silo room floor, and I still hadn't gotten rid of a single one. I decided to reset my cage trap, only this time I moved it about ten feet away from the skunks' hole. I figured if I caught another cat, the skunk wouldn't be as apt to spray it if it was that far away. One thing I must say is that Mr. Stripey never set a foot close to that area again. He had learned his lesson.

We did our daily work around the farm, and that night just before bed we took a flashlight out and checked our trap. Were we in for another big surprise! No, it wasn't a cat this time. Instead, we had two skunks caught in the trap and a third one hanging around the outside of it which I quickly shot. A couple days later we caught the fourth skunk in the trap. Were we ever thankful and blessed to have the unwanted family of skunks gone.

There are things in our lives sometimes that aren't good for us, but we put up with them thinking that they won't hurt us. And they may not hurt us, but they may hurt somebody else. We need to get rid of those things. By doing so, you and those around you will be blessed much more. We are all glad that the skunks are all gone, that includes our cattle and especially Mr. Stripey!

Conclusion

Under an Open Heaven

Y ou, too, can live under an open heaven like we do on our farm here. What do I mean by this, you ask? Where you can wake up daily knowing there is nothing between you and God. Where your sins are confessed and totally forgiven by Him. Where you know He loves you and will guide you throughout the day and bless you. Where you can talk to Him and know that He loves you and will answer your prayers. It is the greatest life possible. I know, for I have lived it for many years now.

The Bible says in Romans 3:23, "For all have sinned, and come short of the glory of God." It goes on to say in Romans 6:23, "For the wages of sin is death; but the gift of God is eternal life through Jesus Christ our Lord." God doesn't want us to go into a fiery hell for all of eternity. So He sent His only Son, Jesus, to die and pay the price for our sins and rebellion so that we could be redeemed to God. So that we could be His children and He could be our loving heavenly Father.

I lived a terrible sinful life before I came to God. But one day I got down on my knees, and with a broken heart cried out to God. He heard me and saved me! He can and will do the same for you if you cry out to Him with all your heart.

Pray, "Father in heaven, I confess that I've sinned against you. Please have mercy on me and forgive me of all of my sins. I confess them unto you now, (name your sins to Him the best you can) and I repent of them. Please forgive me. I believe Jesus died on the cross and was raised from the dead for me. Jesus, please come into my heart and live in me. I give my life fully to You. Thank You, Father, for forgiving me. I commit to live the rest of my life for You. Help me, I pray, in Jesus' name. Amen."

Congratulations. If you have prayed this with all your heart, there's a new name written down in glory and it's yours! Now you too will live under an open heaven. Be sure and read your Bible and pray to Him daily, for when you do, you will find Him. (Jer. 29:13)

You may contact Tom at: <u>lifeonthefamilyfarm@gmail.com</u>

or:

Tom Heck
21079 80th St.
Bloomer, WI 54724

About the Author

Tom Heck, his wife Joanne, and their two children, Catherine and Joshua, own and operate a thirty-five cow, 159-acre dairy farm in northwestern Wisconsin. Tom, having been raised on a dairy farm and now owning his own, shares with his readers the many joys, triumphs and challenges of having a small family farm in the northwoods.

American bush pilot Russell Stendal, on routine business, landed his plane in a remote Colombian village. Gunfire exploded throughout the town and within minutes Russell's 142 day ordeal had begun. The Colombian cartel explained that this was a kidnapping for ransom and that he would be held until payment was made.

Held at gunpoint deep in the jungle and with little else to occupy his time, Russell got ahold of some paper and began to write. He told the story of his life and kept a record of his experience in the guerrilla camp. His "book" became a bridge to the men who held him hostage and now serves as the basis for this incredible true story of how God's love penetrated a physical and ideological jungle.

"My captors tied me up and left the rope on day and night. They were seriously trying to completely break me psychologically and then brainwash me. Every day new things were done to alter me and work towards that goal. My captors started telling me scare stories. Some of these stories were about wild animals. They told me some of the wildest, hair-raising tales about lions and tigers that I have ever heard. These stories were designed both to intimidate me, reducing my ability to sleep, and to cause me to think twice before I decided to try to escape into the jungle again."

This is the story of a 1960s Minnesota mother who struggles to keep up with three small children and housework. Barely able to cope, even with all the modern American conveniences, she panics when her husband begins to talk about pursuing missionary work.

Nothing could have prepared Pat Stendal for her adventure in Christian missions – with mule-riding lessons, sleeping in hammocks in the jungle, and traveling with sick children. A surprise new baby with special physical needs caused Pat to wonder how they would ever manage. Here she was in a new country, needing to learn an entirely new culture while facing overwhelming obstacles – only to learn that the entire time God was simply showing her and her family that His grace is indeed sufficient. And was it ever – their family ministry has been blessed to see thousands of souls won for Christ, and hundreds of thousands of books and Bibles distributed.

jubilee
B I B L E 2000

Hear what God is saying through this original translation

ANEKO Press